Chrissy,
Wishing
you well
Jane

*A SPIRITUAL & PSYCHOLOGICAL APPROACH
TO HEALING EMOTIONAL EATING*

BEYOND THE FOOD GAME

JANE E. LATIMER
Author of *Living Binge-Free*
LivingQuest, Denver

For a free catalog of books and tapes or for ordering information on this book, contact:
LivingQuest Publishing
Box 101412
Denver CO 80250
(303) 789-3980

Cover Design by Bob Schram of Bookends, Boulder
Cover Photograph by Gene Latimer
Illustrations by Jane E. Latimer

Library of Congress Cataloging-in-Publication Data:
Latimer, Jane Evans, 1948-
Beyond the Food Game: a spiritual & psychological approach to healing emotional eating/Jane E. Latimer.
Includes bibliographical references and index.
ISBN 1-882109-01-5; $9.95
1. Compulsive eating—Popular works. 2. Self-help techniques.
I. Title
RC552.C65L3 1993
616.85'26—dc20   93-10052
                                                          CIP

Printed in the United States of America on recycled paper with soy ink.
10 9 8 7 6 5 4 3 2 1

To ensure confidentiality,
all names of clients cited within these pages have been changed.

This book is dedicated to all children and parents.
May we each believe in our innermost Self and seek
the knowledge and skills needed to support
Its unfoldment and expression.

ACKNOWLEDGEMENTS

I sincerely thank the many people who contributed their time, support and feedback to the making of this book: my husband, Gene, for his endless patience and dedication and for all the extra hours he spent parenting when I could not be home; my therapist, David Sawyer, and the IBP trainers and workshop participants who have helped me understand and directly apply these concepts to my personal growth and development; Judy Cole for her role modeling, support and inspiration; Sue and Steve Schwartz for their enduring goodwill through my grumpiest moods and for Sue's exquisite advice; Peter Simmons, my cousin, friend and ally in recovery; the many professionals — Mike Bowers, Barbara Cohn, Nanci Edgecomb, Donna Follansbee, Lindsey Hall, Lee Moyer, Cindy Silvis, Mary Smith, Francie White and Janet Zander — and clients who took time to read the manuscript and give me their invaluable feedback; Bob Schram, my graphic designer, for enabling me to relax and trust in his visual abilities; Anne Higman, my editor; Bob and Lee Evans for their generous financial support; and last, but certainly not least, my children who put up with my long hours away from home.

I am indebted to Jack Rosenberg, Ph.D. and Marjorie Rand, Ph.D., co-founders of the Rosenberg-Rand Institute of Integrative Body Psychotherapy. I express my gratitude to these two highly committed and influential professionals on behalf of myself, my workshop participants, clients and all future emotional eaters whose lives will be touched and helped by their work.

And, of course, I thank all the beautiful people who have sought my professional assistance. For it is they who continue to inspire me to grow and learn — who keep my mind and heart open. I love you all.

CONTENTS

DEEP INSIDE EVEN THE DARKEST MOMENTS, AN EMBER GLOWS.
A SPARK REMAINS. IGNITE THE EMBER WITH LIGHT OF VISION.
FUEL THE FIRE WITH HEALING ENERGY. BURST PRIOR LIMITATIONS.
LOSE WHAT'S FAMILIAR. SWIM IN THE UNFATHOMABLE WATERS OF
UNIVERSAL LIFE-ENERGY AND WONDER, "WHO AM I?"
THE CONCEPTS THAT KEEP US SAFE BUT HALF-DEAD CRUMBLE,
AND IN THEIR PLACE THE SELF IS BORN.

ANYTHING IS POSSIBLE.

PREFACE

I f someone were to tell you it is possible to live a life in which food is not an issue, would you believe them? Probably not, if you live like I did for 20 years: consumed with overeating, dieting, food obsessing, calorie counting and deprivation.

Totally food centered, I isolated myself so people wouldn't interfere with my one and only love — food. The swing shift at work enabled me to rummage through trash-cans looking for leftover lunches thrown away by daytime employees. Exercising up to six hours a day kept my weight at a normal level, even though I often found myself waking from a deep sleep in the middle of the night to stuff an already stuffed stomach when no one would notice.[1] I sacrificed my life for food and I prayed for help. I tried to believe that tomorrow would be different. Tomorrow I'd be thin and normal. Tomorrow I'd be able to eat the way my friends did. Regardless of what I tried to believe, the fact of the matter was my life was totally out of control when it came to food. If someone had told me one day I *could* have a life in which food was not an issue, I would have laughed at the absurdity of the statement. I had tried everything and nothing worked.

Today, I am living that miracle. Food is not an issue and has not been since 1981. There is no fear of the problem ever returning. There is no dieting, no weighing, no obsessing, no worrying, no shame about

---

[1]My experience with food would be considered extreme by some. The degree of our symptoms, however, is not the issue. The great majority of people whose creative energy and potential is misdirected by an unhealthy relationship to food function within the socially accepted, culturally sanctioned eating behavior guidelines. Regardless of how extreme or benign your behavior seems, this book can help.

my body. In its place are rich feelings and an abundance of creative energy.

Since the publication of my first book, *Living Binge-Free* (which is my personal story and guide to recovery), I've dedicated my life to helping other compulsive eaters become free from the obsession that has ruled their lives. Although workshops and individual therapy processes derived from my own healing experiences had become the basis of The Center for Healing Emotional Eating[2] in Denver, it wasn't until I attended a professional workshop given by Marjorie Rand, Ph.D., on Integrative Body Psychotherapy (IBP) that I found an explanation that adequately addressed the "out-of-control" experience of the overeater.[3]

"This is it!" I thought to myself. "This explains why I gorged myself sick for 20 years. This explains how I was able to recover."

Immediately, I took the material and started adapting it for my clients. At workshops, the response was overwhelming. This explanation worked for everyone. My clients said: "Now it makes sense. This is the first time anyone has ever totally understood, described and explained why I have no willpower when it comes to food."

For years up to this point, I had been addressing shame — the underlying feeling that one is not good enough — to explain the emotional triggers of overeating. While important and helpful, focusing on shame did not seem to address adequately the lack of willpower that most compulsive eaters face. Consequently, I had no way to help my clients get a handle on their loss of control. I had no systematic way to help them regain their center and feel whole again.

The out-of-control experience can be devastating. It intensifies whatever shame we already feel, because it proves once again that we are incapable of functioning like others. To the extent we find ourselves losing control around food (or anything else for that matter), we feel powerless.

---

[2] Formerly called the Living Binge-Free Center.
[3] This workshop addressed the childhood injuries of abandonment and invasion, the character styles developed in response to the injury and the fragmentation that occurs when the character style fails. These will be discussed in later chapters.

Some people binge daily, sometimes several times a day. Others, who do not think of themselves as binge eaters, consistently eat too much food or food that is unhealthy or unsatisfying. Others read diet-books, count calories, restrict their food intake or obsess about food incessantly. This behavior, too, can be debilitating. Regardless of how one abuses food, the powerlessness caused by these debilitating patterns can seep into all areas of life, allowing only a mere fraction of one's potential to manifest. The 12 steps of Overeaters Anonymous address the issue of powerlessness in the first step: "We admitted we were powerless over food — that our lives had become unmanageable." Later steps look to a higher power to reinstate sanity. While I have personally experienced the accelerated healing of working with a higher power (addressed specifically in the pages that follow), my experience tells me that, *depending on the way higher power is perceived*, one's belief can either reinforce a sense of powerlessness or not. What I have sought both personally and professionally is a different empowerment process, one that works through opening oneself to a *healing* power which can be accessed *experientially* regardless of whether or not one *believes* in a higher power.

The ideas presented in this book combine psychological *and* spiritual perspectives which specifically address the out-of-control experience of emotional eating. (The term "emotional eating" refers to all behavioral and mental patterns of eating, restricting and obsessing experienced by the individual as undesirable, destructive or unwanted and which the individual feels helpless to change.) These ideas are derived from 18 years of personal and professional healing experiences. Although I had already formulated my own concepts of the recovery process based on these experiences, when I became acquainted with IBP, founded by Jack Rosenberg, Ph.D. and Marjorie Rand, Ph.D., the many details of this process were put in place. The contributions of Rosenberg and Rand can be found in Chapters Three, Four and Seven, which describe character styles, fragmentation and boundary development as presented in their training and book, *Body, Self and Soul*.[4]

---

[4]Jack Rosenberg, Ph. D., Marjorie Rand, Ph.D. and Diane Asay, M.A., *Body, Self and Soul: Sustaining Integration* (Atlanta: Humanics Limited, 1985).

These concepts address injuries and traumas that occur in every child's life and which block awareness of and unfoldment of the true Self. Emotional eating is most always triggered by events or chronic life situations that remind us of our unmet childhood needs. These triggers provide us with a great opportunity for healing. The healing method described here may include the invitation of assistance from a higher power or simply from an inner loving aspect of ourselves.

Whichever way you choose, it is my hope that *Beyond the Food Game* will help you to begin utilizing your own healing and body powers to create a strong, healthy Self and to proceed on this journey of Self-unfoldment with new understanding, compassion and love.

Beyond the Food Game offers a single important perspective on healing emotional eating. For additional specific behavioral and cognitive interventions that may be necessary, refer to the resources listed on pages 123 and 124. Exercises are scattered throughout the text. Reading with a pen and a notebook or journal in hand and doing the exercises as you encounter them will enable greater assimilation of the material. The tools presented here may be used to enhance your own personal journey of recovery — whether that be with a therapist, support group, hospital treatment program, 12 Step program or work of your own design. When used consistently and in combination with ideas presented in my other books, these tools can empower you to release your food addiction. Armed with new insight and implementation of the practical step-by-step methods outlined herein, you will be able to regain control of your life and food, and to feel good and whole again.

CHAPTER ONE

The Food Game

MYSTICS AND SAGES THROUGH THE CENTURIES HAVE MAINTAINED THAT HUMAN EXISTENCE IS BUT A VAST ARENA IN WHICH THE INDIVIDUAL SOUL EVOLVES, BY MEETING AN ENDLESS SERIES OF CHALLENGES. PAIN IS THE GAUGE THAT INDICATES THERE IS AN ASPECT OF OUR LIFE THAT NEEDS ATTENTION — THAT REQUIRES US TO LET GO, MOVE FORWARD, TAKE A RISK, MAKE A "SHIFT IN CONSCIOUSNESS."

WE ARE BORN INTO A CULTURE THAT GOES TO GREAT LENGTHS TO STOP PAIN AS QUICKLY AND CONVENIENTLY AS POSSIBLE. FEW OF US ARE EVER ENCOURAGED TO BE WITH OUR PAIN. MORE OFTEN, THE PREVAILING ADVICE IS TO COVER IT UP, DEADEN IT, LEAVE IT BEHIND. WE SIT GLAZED IN FRONT OF THE TV WATCHING THE FANTASY LIVES OF OTHERS, IGNORING THE INNER DEPTHS OF OUR OWN. MILLIONS CONSUME SEDATIVES AND PAIN-KILLERS AS A DAILY STAPLE. MANY OF US IN RECENT GENERATIONS ARE BORN INTO THIS WORLD DRUGGED. FREQUENTLY, WE ARE NUMB TO THE BIRTH OF OUR OWN CHILDREN. WE USUALLY LEAVE LIFE DRUGGED AS WELL. MOST OF US MISS ALL THE MAJOR LIFE PASSAGES BECAUSE OUR SENSES ARE DULLED IN AN ATTEMPT TO AVOID PAIN.

5

WE HAVE INHERITED A WORLD VIEW THAT DOES NOT ENCOURAGE US TO LOOK BEHIND THE SURFACE OF ISSUES. OUR OFFICIAL MEDICINE TREATS THE SYMPTOMS OF DISEASE, WHILE GENERALLY IGNORING THE MORE DEMANDING SEARCH FOR UNDERLYING CAUSES. TELEVISION HYPNOTIZES US WITH A PARADE OF VISUAL AND SOUND "BITES" — ALL SHOW AND LITTLE SUBSTANCE. UNLIKE TRADITIONAL CULTURES, WE HAVE CREATED VIRTUALLY NO MEANINGFUL INITIATIONS OR RITES OF PASSAGE THAT PENETRATE BENEATH APPEARANCES AND ADDRESS OUR TRUE NEEDS: PERSONAL GROWTH AND EVOLUTION.

WE'VE CREATED WHAT NO TRADITIONAL CULTURE EVER HAD: AN ALMOST UNIVERSALLY ADDICTED AND/OR ALIENATED POPULATION, CEASELESSLY ANESTHETIZING AND DIVERTING ITSELF WITH EXTERNAL SUBSTANCES AND ACTIVITIES. WE CONSTANTLY STRIVE TO ERECT AND MAINTAIN OUR OWN "GREAT WALL" AGAINST THE VOID WITHIN US. WE BEAT BACK UNWANTED FEELINGS AND MEMORIES, PAIN AND STRESS, TEMPORARILY SLAYING THEM WITH ALCOHOL, DRUGS, FOOD OR WHATEVER WORKS.

All the while I was overeating there was a child inside calling for help. "Love me," she'd whisper in my ear as I reached for the ice-cream in the freezer. I didn't hear her because I wasn't looking for her. I didn't know there was a message hidden within this addiction because no one had alerted me to this simple fact.

Mary[1] is a yo-yo dieter. Her happiness depends upon her ability to stay in control of her food cravings. When Mary loses weight, she feels in control of herself, motivated and successful. But, in order to maintain her state of empowerment, she has to adhere to strict food guidelines; she eats only 1,200 calories a day and spends most of her time and energy overriding thoughts of food — thoughts which consume her every waking moment. Inevitably, she gives in to her cravings. From the moment she breaks her diet (a Big Mac and fries, perhaps), she loses control. Becoming more and more withdrawn, she isolates herself in her apartment until she is able to muster the willpower needed to get back on her diet.

As long as Mary is dieting, she is able to stay in control of her feelings, her food and her life. Dieting keeps Mary on a "high." As long as she is obsessed with losing weight, she will never deal with the underlying emptiness and powerlessness caused by her *inability to connect with her real feelings and needs*. It is these core issues and her unwillingness to confront them that cause Mary to be both a player and chronic loser of the food game.

Abe grew up on a farm. "Mealtimes were family times — the only time we did anything other than work. I've been on many diets and lost weight but the thought of another diet makes me sick. I can't tolerate being hungry. Yet, I can't stand the extra 75 pounds I am carrying." Because meals are associated with love and togetherness, Abe is driven to override his own body wisdom. Eating too much of the wrong foods on a daily basis adversely affects his health, energy and state of well-being.

---

[1]Although overeating is a problem effecting both men and women, because the majority of people actively seeking help with this are women (and because most of my clients are women), I have chosen for the most part to use female case examples, as well as the female pronouns (she, her). With all due respect to my male readers and clients, this in no way reflects a gender prejudice on my part.

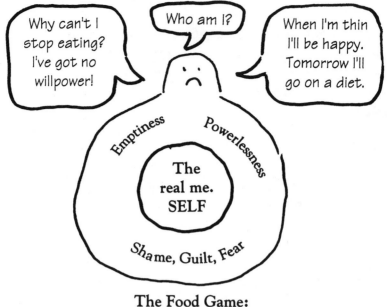

The Food Game:
Dieting, Obsessing, Weighing, Bingeing, Overeating

Sally, mother of three, has just lost 55 pounds on a liquid diet. In a marriage with little communication and no support, she feels discounted, alone and powerless to change her situation. "We start eating real food again tomorrow. I'm petrified," she cries. "I don't know how to eat like a normal person. What will I do?" Sally's inability to meet her own needs keeps her spinning on a binge/diet treadmill.

Betsy, a 25 year old grade school teacher, is a lovely, bright, ambitious and caring young woman. Yet, Betsy has a terrible secret. She is bulimic. "The bingeing starts when I get home from school. I go through all the food in the house, then throw it up in the toilet. I feel ashamed but am powerless to change. I keep hoping it will go away but I know it won't." Like many bulimics, Betsy uses her drive to succeed and food addiction to cover up underlying feelings of unworthiness.

Jan is approaching her desired weight. "I feel overwhelmed and on the verge of bingeing. It's scary without my fat. All I want to do is eat and gain weight. Yet, I want to be thin. I'm so confused." Without the weight, Jan must confront the vulnerability she feels around her own sexuality.

The person who plays the food game has an emotionally charged relationship to food — feeling "up" when eating the right foods, at the right time, in the right amounts, and down when eating the wrong foods, at the wrong time, in the wrong amounts. It is precisely this emotional charge that makes food addictive. We become dependent on the mood-altering effects not only of such foods as sugar, but also of the whole complex structure of dieting and overeating. Overeating can help us to avoid our feelings, calm anxiety and uplift depression. Dieting can give us a sense of control. The rules distract us. We measure and weigh, count calories, stay away from "bad" foods and eat only at specified times of the day. Above all, we are instructed not to listen to our bodies (this keeps us blissfully unaware of the uncomfortable sensations we feel), but rather to override our hunger and deny our physical needs. The "high" created by the fantasy that when we are thin we will be happy enables us to rise above the underlying issues.

The winner of the food game successfully loses weight or manages to maintain her already acceptable weight, but is she really winning? The goal of the game is to get the "I'm okay" feeling by changing our eating behaviors. Successful for a time, we feel good about ourselves. But when we have a stressful day or feel deprived and the diet is broken, all the good feelings that were dependent upon our winning disappear. A loser at our own game, we're thrown into the void once more. "What's wrong with me? I have no willpower!" "I'll never be thin. I'll never be happy. It's a losing battle." Our mind races with negative self-talk that reflects the flip side of the high — the powerlessness and shame that separate us from our true Self.

The food game is a *distraction* — an attempt to control the unpleasant feelings caused by our disconnection from Self. We play it to create an illusion of happiness based on "winning" — being thin and sticking to the rules by being "good" with our food. But when we "lose" the game, go off our diet and regain the weight, we are left with our underlying inability to know our Self.

Those of you who have played this game more than once know that winning is nearly impossible. Trying to change food behavior **without addressing the real issues** is a losing battle. When we break a rule, we lose the motivation to continue: "Why bother? I've screwed up! Might as well go all the way." We're back into the food and another round of the game is lost.

Healing requires a willingness on our part to give up the "high." We must abandon the illusion that when we are thin we will be happy — so that we can genuinely feel our experiences. Letting go of the food game may seem scary because we know on some level we will be faced, perhaps for the first time, with an array of uncomfortable feelings, problems which have been previously avoided, and our own poorly defined identity. This realization is crucial, however, because with it comes hope. Once we become aware of the truth of our feelings, problems and needs, we can be empowered to act on our own behalf. Moving steadfastly inward to the center of our Self, we can discover a truly rich and fulfilling life.

CHAPTER TWO

The Self

TO BE ONE'S SELF IS TO ACCEPT ONE'S TALENTS, ONE'S GIFTS, ONE'S ERRORS AND IMPERFECTIONS, ONE'S VISIONS, AND ONE'S WORK. TO BE AT PEACE IS TO EXPERIENCE ONE'S SELF FROM THE PERSPECTIVE OF THE WHOLE, WHICH IS MUCH LARGER AND MUCH GREATER THAN THE SELF CAN EVER BE — TO BE SURRENDERED TO ONE'S TINY AND SIMPLE, YET UNIQUE, PLACE ON EARTH.

There was once a time when the human child was lulled to blissful sleep in the warm embrace of soft skin at mother's breast. Sweet, white nectar soothed the aching feeling in our bellies. Warm skin soothed the coldness.

Food now recreates that blissful time. The pain of life-struggle disappears temporarily as we eat ourselves to sleep. But the struggle continues and excess food makes us fat. We hate what we are doing to ourselves. "Where am I? What am I doing? Where is my life?" We realize that our obsession with food demands a terrible self-sacrifice. Lost and trapped within its clutches, we cry for help. "Let me out," the true Self cries in a soft little voice.

"What is that I hear?"

"It is your Self."

"Who are you?"

"I am your lost Self."

"How do I find you?"

"Follow your instincts."

"What?"

"Follow your instincts."

"But where are my instincts?"

"They are here, buried deep under layers of feelings of unworthiness and protections from feeling. They are buried here below your fear and fat and stuffing."

"What?"

"Stop overeating. Food is not the way."

"What?"

"Stop dieting. Dieting will not bring you to me. Look for me in your feelings. Look for me in your spirit."

"What?"

"Good-bye."

"What? Where are you? Don't leave me! Come back. Come back. Come back."

T he raw material with which we came into this world was filled with promise. We came ready to receive joy, ready to take on the challenges of life's glorious journey. We came eager to receive the skills and tools which would enable us to express our love, unique gifts and talents to the world. We came prepared to give and receive love, to express ourselves and enjoy the gifts of others, and to grow and learn.

Our birth was a promise. To the extent our parents, friends and society were and are still *unable* to support this promise, the insides of our soul, our Self, has and is being stifled, lost.[1]

This unfulfilled promise creates a festering hunger. The loss is unspeakable. The grief erodes a hole so vast that no amount of food, people, money, work or anything outside can fill its bottomless pit. Yet, no matter how traumatic our childhood, no matter how cut off we are from our awareness of this promise, there is a part of us that is in touch with it. We all know this because it is part of our humanity. We cannot be human without knowing on some deep level that we are connected to the creative and healing power of life which flows through us like a river. Some may call this source God; others, spirit, higher power or higher self. Some experience it in nature. Yet, it is my belief that all of us are connected to this power and that it is our *experience* of it on all levels — mental, emotional and physical — that creates this aliveness which I call the Self.

My search for Self began when I sought to heal myself from a twenty-year, debilitating eating disorder and generally miserable life. I was raised in a tiny two bedroom apartment in New York City and shared a room with my sister.

"Goddamn it, Lisa, stop the practicing now!" The drumming contin-ues a few yards from the dining room table. I cringe. Here we go again. Immersed in the rat-a-tat-tat of sticks on drums, she is oblivious to the desperate demands of our father, who wishes only to eat his dinner in peace.

---

[1]This statement is not meant to blame any one person, force or condition. In many ways we are all victims of a rampant cultural dis-ease that idolizes drama, appearance and material acquisition at the expense of inner qualities, (i.e., reflec-tion, intuition, gentleness and stillness) badly needed for Self unfoldment.

Mom cries. I sit there helpless. Those sounds pierce my ears, too. "Which is worse?" I wonder, "the drums, the yelling or the crying?"

Dad bolts upright, throws his napkin down and storms about. Lisa refuses to budge. Now the obstinate expression on her face is more apparent. If it could speak, it would say, "Hey! You screwed up — so take this!" One punch, then another — BANG, POW, BANG as the sticks hit the drum.

Mom and Dad were products of a society in which anger, rage, emptiness and grief are buried under facades of glamor and perfection. Society teaches us how to "succeed," not how to listen to the feelings of our children. Like those of so many other kids, my growing pains were ignored. My parents just didn't know how to listen. If I was angry or upset, Mom felt guilt and became defensive. So I gave up. So, it seemed to me, did Lisa. She used her drums to yell and scream. I used overeating. I also used school to drown my feelings. With "A's," I got the strokes I so badly needed. I learned to squelch my needs, feelings, fears — all my inadequacies — under a mask of perfection and addiction to food.

When I left home, I fell apart. As desperate as I was to appear perfect, there was no getting around the fact that I was totally out of control around food. Like many other young troubled women who move directly from parents to partner, I hooked up with a "super-man," living in his world — his friends, his values, his needs. He was supposed to love me, care for me, support me financially and emotionally — fill me up and make me whole. That was his use to me. Meanwhile, he used me. I was his plaything and when he got bored, he dropped me like a broken toy with half the pieces missing. I shattered.

When he left, I fell apart. I felt as if I had nothing — no love, no caring, no support — only food to fill the loneliness. It was within this context of dysfunction that I unconsciously and frantically searched for something to give my life meaning, to hold me together, to show me a way back to the essence of my being.

Young children are innately in touch with their essence. They are vulnerable and open to experience — feeling and sensing without inhibition. They express their unique gifts, talents and characteristics spontaneously and joyously. Our childhood environment has great influence upon the fate of the Self. For many of us, our maturing personality retains little of our vulnerability and unique gifts, as our personality develops into a complex structure of characteristics designed to ensure our survival and acceptance.

Unfortunately, as is true for almost all of us, I lost contact with my Self as I grew out of childhood and became more and more identified with the rules and expectations that others placed on my existence. Soon, my sense of Self existed as little more than a vague memory or sense of things not being right.

As a child I remember being acutely aware of the empty masks posing as adults which seemed so alienated from life energy. My aliveness turned to rage as I felt myself being squelched by my parents and environment. Yet still a child, enmeshed in a fantasy that "they must be right, I must be wrong," the rage too was squelched as I turned to food to numb me out, dull my sensations, feelings and perceptions. Through my addiction to food I, too, became a mask and learned to survive in a world hostile to my essential nature. As the years went by, "I" became identified with my dysfunctional behavior. Only after years of inner work did I begin to understand that this compulsive self was merely a false personality that had nothing to do with my essence.

I wake up with a start. The afternoon sun glares through the windows that face the West Side Highway. "Oh God, what time is it?" I think. I fish for the clock, buried under old clothes and paint brushes. "4:09" it reads.

My chest heaves. I look around. "What now?" I think. "Don't see Dr. Cranendonck until tomorrow." I think about some cheese. "Sounds good, but if I put it off, could lose some weight."

I'm trying to ward off the deep hole inside — the blackness that is cruelly set off by the contrasting brightness coming in through those damn windows. "Will night ever come?" I think. The darkness feels better to me. I come alive then — darkness within, without, resonating in perfect pitch.

"Dread, dread, go away
Please don't come another day."
I find myself starting to draw. Poems usually accompany my drawings

these days. Although in my mid-twenties, silly childlike images adorn my pads.

Acutely aware of the void, I sought new ways to open to my life force, realizing on some level that the void could only be filled by this force. I found myself withdrawing from outer attachments — going within. The thrust to manifest my Self became so strong that it literally smashed the constraints of my conditioning.

This came in stages. Amidst the despair, I began to have a pronounced series of awakenings.

One such event occurred as I boarded the downtown subway for home one afternoon after a Rolfing[2] session. Suddenly and without warning I felt a strong power. I was planted in a new world of infinite love and peace. The emptiness was gone — so was the darkness and despair. In their place was an awesome Presence — flowing within and without — bathing me in a crystalline consciousness. Senses peaked. My mind was clear. Energy radiated everywhere. My life was imbued with power. The mysterious had become a reality. A light pierced my despair, penetrating the darkness for but a few hours but profoundly affecting my perception of reality.[3]

Despite this experience, my life was still largely unmanageable. Although I was aware of this force, I was living in a body that felt, thought, perceived and acted in its old conditioned ways. I had moments of deep insight and occasional feelings of well-being, but they were quickly followed by the old emotional and mental garbage dragging me down.

My "peak" experience became a touchstone — a glimpse of potential — that stayed to guide me as I pursued a new but relentless goal: to feel that power manifesting in my life *on a daily basis*. Time passed. The darkness and pain returned. So did my dysfunctional

---

[2]Rolfing is a form of bodywork designed to release defensive holding patterns in the body. For more information, see Resources, p. 123.

[3]Not all awakenings are so extreme. Most often, awakenings occur slowly. This can be achieved through self-searching and daily practice in programs which utilize mindfulness, meditation or prayer. Some helpful programs that I know of are Ira Progoff's Intensive Journal, A Course in Miracles and the 12-Step recovery programs.

behavior. But through it all, from that time forward, I knew that I could be more. I just didn't know how I was going to make that goal a reality.

I wake up this morning with a sickness deep inside. Something dark, insidious, comes in on me and causes me to hate my life. The pain gnaws at my solar plexus. I close my eyes and reach deep inside. I travel with my awareness into the pain. It intensifies. My mind is racing, the pain is gnawing my insides, my mind is working furiously, remembering. Then in a flash, I understand.

This realization was a turning point — the point at which I knew I had to meet head-on the darkness that resided within. This *void* that I experienced — a pit of emptiness — had to be dealt with if I was to sustain my recovery, for it was precisely this void that held the key to my fulfillment.

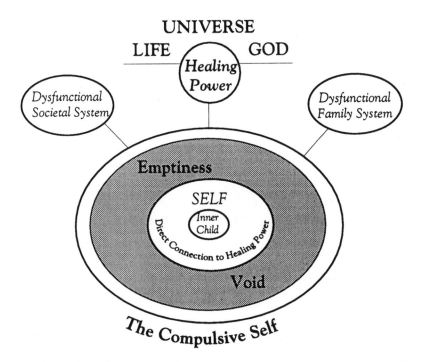

I drew this chart one afternoon in an attempt to communicate clearly what I had experienced as I journeyed through the void.

The outer circle represents the compulsive self — the part that is formed as a result of the family and social forces acting upon us. I like to think of this compulsive self as a protective covering — a kind of makeshift replacement — an *adaptive self* that has been built to ensure our survival while living in an environment hostile to the unfoldment of the Self. **It is the compulsive self that plays the food game.**

The Self, depicted by the inner circle, lives in the present and is in touch with and appropriately expresses its authentic feelings and needs. It is alive and open to experience, holding the specific talents, gifts and traits with which we are endowed. The middle section — the void — reflects the areas in which the growth of this Self is blocked. It is experienced as a hole or emptiness — a kind of half-put-together jigsaw puzzle with pieces missing.

Healing takes place as we begin to become aware that who we have been, how we have functioned, no longer works. Trouble with relationships, money, unfulfilling work or major life transitions such as moving our place of residence, death of a loved one or sickness can reveal the inadequacy of the adaptive self to truly meet our needs. Life is a powerful teacher. As we mature, periods of unhappiness may become more difficult to disguise as we are confronted with the looming inevitability of our own mortality and the reality of wasted years. We begin to experience a breakdown of the compulsive self. The food game becomes more and more difficult to play. The pain increases as more and more holes are punctured through this protective shell.

Some of us are lucky enough to discover that the *way out* of the void is by going *through* it to the center. Unfortunately, most of us are not aware of this option. We get lost in the void, then grope our way back to that which feels familiar, only to find that our compulsive self becomes less and less reliable.

CHAPTER THREE

The Injured Self

IN MANY WAYS THE SELF IS POWERLESS AND
MUST OBEY THE LAWS OF THE UNIVERSE. IF THE
INDIVIDUAL DISOBEYS THOSE LAWS, HE SUFFERS
THE CONSEQUENCES. SO, IT BEHOOVES ONE TO
UNDERSTAND, TO LISTEN, TO INTUIT, TO KNOW
WHAT THOSE LAWS ARE.

"Janie, would you like the light turned on?" *"No, Mother,"* I say under my breath. The insides of my gut feel like a volcano about to explode. My throat is tight. Every muscle is taut with rage as my body relives childhood feelings of suffocation.

I think back on the past four days. "Only four days a year, Jane. You can do it. Keep up the smile. Be the good daughter for only a few more hours. Then you will be on the plane, going back home to the life you have built." I say this to myself. I try to talk myself into making it through the holidays, but I don't. I don't make it without the fight. I start it, as usual. I find something wrong and explode. After an exchange of hostile words, my father and I try to come to terms, but I know that things are not right. I recede again within my shell while the shame of not being the daughter they wanted engulfs me.

Stepping onto the airplane with my two sons, I wonder how much of our inability to communicate is my fault and how much of it is theirs. I have the next five hours of this flight from Boca Raton to Denver to try to understand and sort out what has just happened. I have the rest of my life to sort out and understand the depth of confusion, anger, despair and grief I have always felt.

Psychologists who study the relationship of the developmental process to the unfolding of a strong and positive Self agree that the fate of this Self is dependent upon the parents' ability , to 1) nurture the child 2) reflect the child's feelings and needs (especially when different from that of the parents), 3) respond to the child's needs, and 4) set appropriate limits.[1]

Whenever one of these conditions is lacking, and to the degree that it is lacking, the child suffers a comparable *injury* to its healthy Self formation, much as the lack of proper nutrients would injure the child's physical development. Because the word "injury" can have a strong negative connotation and often results in the blaming of the parent, I wish to emphasize here that all individuals receive a mix of good and bad parenting. Parenting skills are passed down through the generations. Most parents do the best they can. To blame the parent for our injuries is nearsighted and unfruitful. Most parents affect the development of the child's Self in both negative and positive ways.

When a Self is formed adequately, we say it has good *boundaries*; that is, has a strong sense of feelings and needs as *separate, as good as* and *equal to* the feelings and needs of others. The child has a strong and positive self-image that holds up under the challenges and stressors of life circumstance. When any or all of the conditions needed for healthy Self development are lacking, we say the child is either abandoned, invaded or both. In fact, because all psychological injuries are the result of some degree of abandonment and/or invasion and *all* children are injured, the coping style of each individual is formed, in part, in response to the degree and frequency of these injuries. If the injury happens often enough, the Self recoils — receding deep within a protective shell (its adaptive self) until the day it is liberated, under the proper conditions.

Abandonment is an absence of adequate love, caring or presence. A child can be abandoned in a variety of ways and to different degrees.

---

[1]See Thomas Paris, Ph.D. and Eileen Paris, Ph.D. *"I'll Never Do To My Kids What My Parents Did to Me!": A Guide to Conscious Parenting* (Los Angeles: Lowell House, 1992); Dorothy Corkille Briggs, *Your Child's Self-Esteem* (New York: Dolphin Books, 1970); D.N. Stern, *The Interpersonal World of the Infant* (New York: Basic Books, 1985).

An absence of physical presence or touch may be one form of abandonment, but I have seen people who felt abandoned even with the physical presence of the parent. Most often it is the emotional presence that is lacking. A parent may be there but 'not there' — distracted, empty, busy, overwhelmed, judgmental, and so on. Whenever a child is not seen or heard objectively or accurately, there is a degree of abandonment regardless of whether the parent is physically present or not.

Invasion, on the other hand, is an overpowering of the child's feelings and needs through control, manipulation and disrespect. (Setting appropriate limits is very different from invading a child's space. Limit setting should always take place in an atmosphere of love, understanding and respect.) Invasive behavior invalidates the child's feelings and needs and communicates to the child that she is unworthy and incapable of knowing her Self and making her own decisions. Any non-verbal, verbal or physical behavior that overpowers or is shaming or disrespectful to the child is invasive.[2]

One of the parenting skills needed for healthy development of a separate Self is *mirroring*. The parent must be able to stand back and see his or her child's feelings, thoughts, values and behaviors objectively, putting her own feelings aside in that moment. The act of mirroring is a four-fold process. It entails *listening, acknowledging, validating* and *responding* in a manner appropriate to the child's feelings and needs. Jesse and Cory (our two sons) play well together most of the time but, as is to be expected, have regular conflicts around such very important issues as who gets his apple *first*, or who gets the *red* plate, or who gets to have his book read *first*.

On the days I do my job well, I might say, "It sure is important to you both who gets the apple first," (I'm listening, acknowledging and validating their values) "and it makes you angry when the other one gets it first and you don't" (I'm listening, acknowledging and vali-

---

[2]For a more complete description of abandonment and invasion, see *Body, Self and Soul*, op. cit., John Bradshaw, *Bradshaw on: The Family* (Deerfield Beach: Health Communications, 1988) and *Healing the Shame that Binds You* (Deerfield Beach: Health Communications, 1988); Alice Miller, *The Drama of the Gifted Child* (New York: Basic Books, 1981).

dating their feelings). "Dealing with that feeling by crying and yelling might not get you the results you want. When you yell like that, I don't feel like giving you anything." (I respond to their behavior by showing them how their behavior affects my feelings.) "How else can you work it out?" I've trained my sons to work out their differences by coming up with options that both can accept. So, this approach can work much of the time. In this way I respond to their needs by reminding them of alternative behaviors that might serve these needs more efficiently.

If I'm having a good day — centered and peaceful — I can mirror my children well. This shows each one his own values and feelings while also giving him a sense of his behavior and how it affects the feelings of others. They each learn "I am a separate individual from my parents and siblings with things that are important to me and feelings that are mine." This awareness is how a child develops his Self. He also becomes aware that "screaming upsets my mother and doesn't get me what I want." This is how a child develops an awareness of another's Self.

Through the parent's accurate mirroring, the child sees an image of herself, just as if she were actually looking into a mirror. This helps the child form a positive self-image which is separate, as good as and equal to other selves. When this happens, the Self develops a healthy boundary.

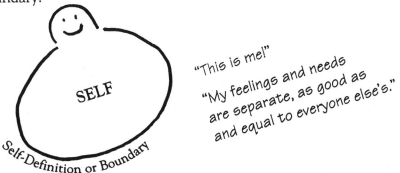

SELF

Self-Definition or Boundary

"This is me!"

"My feelings and needs are separate, as good as and equal to everyone else's."

If the parent mirrors inaccurately or not at all, the child doesn't learn to distinguish herself from others and either forms a distorted self-image ("I am a selfish person," "I am a bad person," "I am a stupid person") or none at all ("I don't exist," "I don't deserve to be heard or seen"). Because these distortions make it difficult to function as an adult, an adaptive self is formed. The purpose of the adaptive self is to enable us to feel good enough about ourselves to carry on. The adaptive self attempts to give us the "I'm okay" experience.

To truly experience our Self is to be in the present. The adaptive self holds *old* feelings and operates from *old* motives. Thus, the more you are able to relax and be open in the moment, to feel joy, sadness, hurt, or anger as these relate to a present situation, the greater your ability to stand in the center of your Self.

> "I get my self-definition from the people I'm with, the activities I do, or the rules and expectations I live with."

The Injured Self

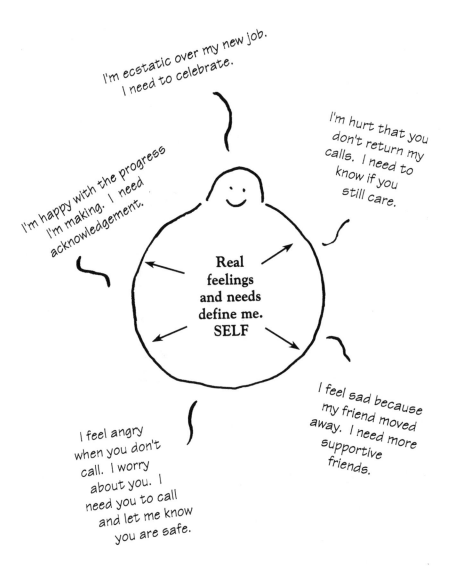

I'm ecstatic over my new job. I need to celebrate.

I'm hurt that you don't return my calls. I need to know if you still care.

I'm happy with the progress I'm making. I need acknowledgement.

Real feelings and needs define me. SELF

I feel sad because my friend moved away. I need more supportive friends.

I feel angry when you don't call. I worry about you. I need you to call and let me know you are safe.

"I get my self-definition from feelings and needs experienced in the present."

The Healthy Self

What is Self-Definition?

As you can see, when we are mirrored accurately, we retain an accurate picture of our feelings, needs and values and they become our self-image or definition.

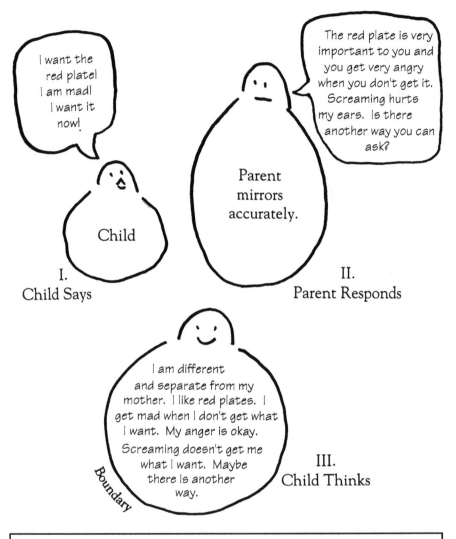

I want the red plate! I am mad! I want it now!

The red plate is very important to you and you get very angry when you don't get it. Screaming hurts my ears. Is there another way you can ask?

Parent mirrors accurately.

Child

I.
Child Says

II.
Parent Responds

I am different and separate from my mother. I like red plates. I get mad when I don't get what I want. My anger is okay. Screaming doesn't get me what I want. Maybe there is another way.

Boundary

III.
Child Thinks

Johnny looks in the mirror and sees himself reflected in his mother's image. He sees his own values and feelings reflected back to him and in this way forms an accurate self-definition.

When we are not mirrored accurately, we do not retain our feelings, needs and values and thereby lose an accurate self-image or definition.

Johnny looks in the mirror and sees that something is wrong with him. He forms an image of himself as unworthy.

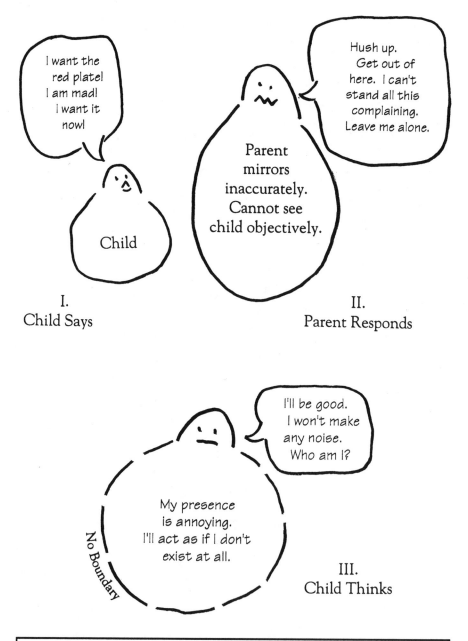

Johnny looks in the mirror and sees that others would be happier without him. He sees himself disappear. He grows up to deny his own feelings and needs.

Self-definition is a boundary. It is an internal (body) experience of our feelings, needs and values as *separate, as good as* and *equal* to others' feelings, needs and values. The experience of being without a boundary is highly disconcerting, so we create definition in other ways: 1) by looking to people and/or food for definition (The Never Enougher); 2) by creating rigid rules around food and body weight and/or creating rigid body structure, i.e., excessively thin or fat. (The Super Trooper); and 3) by splitting off from the body — living from the head up (The As Iffer).[3]

The way an emotional eater creates definition will be determined by the particular type of injury she suffered as a child. A particular style may predominate or all three styles may exist equally within the individual. Let's take an in-depth look at each.

Looking Outside for Definition — The "Never Enougher"

"Larry hasn't called in 3 days. Feel choked and scared, empty. Want to eat, eat, eat. Noticed Laura and her friend. How bouncy and happy she is. What's wrong with me? Why am I never loved?" (Journal, 1974)

Sally's attempts at self-expression overwhelmed her mom. "I was the fifth of eight children. There was so much going on, so much activity, that no one seemed to notice me. I learned to sit in a corner and play with my dolls or color and read. I was the good kid." Because Sally's needs increased her mother's burden, Sally learned to suppress her own needs, her Self, in order to win her mother's approval. Because her true feelings and needs have not been heard and validated, her connection with Self is lost. She feels empty. She carries within her a longing for recognition, acknowledgement and validation. This emptiness causes her to look to outside objects to try to get the experience of Self-validation that is missing. Anything can be used to fill this hole — people, food, work, money. But because she looks to external sources to fill the emptiness, there will *never* be *enough* people, food, work or money to fill it and the longings will be

---

[3]Character Styles (Never Enougher, Super Trooper and As Iffer) are from IBP training and *Body, Self and Soul.* They are adapted here for emotional eaters.

experienced again and again. Sally's underlying belief is "I'm not okay without _____ (a person, a job, food, money, etc.)."

The "Never Enougher" has no Self-boundary. She gets her definition through the object she has *attached* herself to — food, relationship, career.

Food, relationships, work or money can define the Never Enougher's identity.

Many Never Enoughers *have* to be in relationships in order to feel good about themselves and will do *anything* to keep the relationship, including perpetuating the pattern of Self-denial. Because their feelings and needs were not mirrored accurately as children, they learn to distrust themselves. Because they don't know their own feelings and needs, they need others to define them. Their greatest fear is that of abandonment because if they are abandoned they lose their self-definition — and when this happens they feel as if they are falling apart. This "falling apart" experience is a replication of what it felt like as a child not to be seen, heard or reflected. Without mirroring, the child cannot hold an image of herself and the experience is one of self-obliteration. Self-obliteration can be experienced as severe anxiety, shame, rage, fear, panic. It is a loss of Self-definition and can feel as if one is trying to stay afloat in the ocean of life without a life preserver.

The Never Enougher: Parent can't respond to child's real needs.

One client, Missy, feels comfortable with me sitting very close to her in our sessions. When I move across the room, however, she feels anxious. It becomes clear to us both, as we work, that Missy has no boundary. She attaches to others, hoping to fill the deep longing she feels inside — hoping to get an experience of her Self. The closer people are, the safer she feels. The further I move away, the greater anxiety she feels because my distance reminds her of the way it felt as a child. When, as children, we don't have someone to mirror our feelings and needs, it feels as if we don't exist. The adult serves as both a role model and a container for the child's Self until the child is old enough to hold that Self in its own container. If the child does not have the adult as a container, it never forms its own container and continues to seek others to create a container for its still unformed Self. Missy, in effect, needs my closeness to help contain her. She needs other people to help her "stay together." Others become her definition, and when they try to distance themselves from her, it feels as if she is disintegrating. Because Missy doesn't have a boundary, the more others try to separate, the greater the experience of disintegrating — it is as if she is floating in that ocean of nothingness. Then, she turns to food to anchor her.

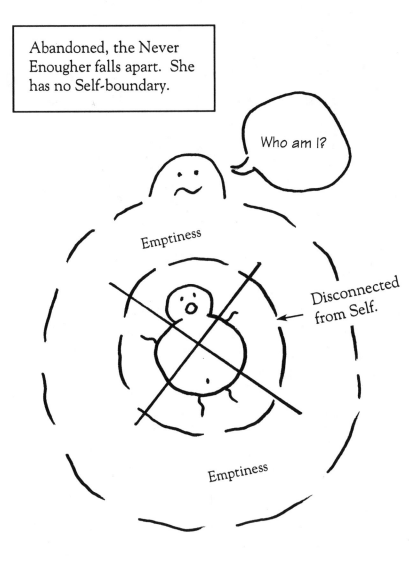

Abandoned, the Never Enougher falls apart. She has no Self-boundary.

Because the real feelings were never mirrored and the real needs were never met, the real Self is obliterated.

Never Enoughers eat for three reasons: 1) to anchor themselves — give themselves a boundary; 2) to fill the emptiness and longing caused by repressed feelings and needs; and 3) to ease the anxiety caused by fear of not getting or losing the love and recognition they long for.

If you think you may eat for any of the above reasons, you probably have high abandonment anxiety. Most emotional eaters have Never Enougher qualities to one degree or another.

Check this out by answering the following questions:

- Do I use food to fill an emptiness, neediness or longing?
- Do I feel anxious, upset, tense or uncomfortable when others want some distance from me?
- Do I use food to soothe or escape from my uncomfortable feelings?
- Has eating been triggered by feelings of rejection?
- Would I rather be with people than be alone?
- Can I handle my food better when in a relationship?
- Did I feel abandoned or neglected as a child?
- Has the onset of my eating disorder correlated with loss of a loved one?

If you have answered yes to any of these questions, you probably have some Never Enougher characteristics. You may find it helpful to take some time to write about specific incidents.

Now, close your eyes. Remember a time when you were a child and felt abandoned in any way. Perhaps you were actually left alone. Or, perhaps you tried to talk to a parent but he or she didn't hear you, or discounted what you said, or didn't believe you, or didn't care.

Perhaps you felt that your siblings or others had more time with your parents than you did. Perhaps you weren't clothed, fed or given adequate medical attention. In whatever way you felt abandoned, take some time to remember how this was for you. Open your eyes and answer the following questions:

- How did I feel?
- What did I do with the feelings?
- Did I express them?
- Did I hold them back?

- How did I cope with abandonment?
- Do I feel similarly today?
- How do I cope today?
- Does food play a part in my coping style?
- Do people, work, sex or money play a part in my coping style?

Notice, if at any time in recent months, you have binged, overeaten or obsessed about food as a result of feeling abandoned. If you have, reconnect with that out-of-control feeling and ask yourself the following questions:

- Do I feel as if I am falling apart?
- Do I feel as if I can't function?
- Do I feel overwhelmed?
- Am I scared?
- Can I focus?
- Do I feel as if I am trying to swim in an ocean with no land in sight?

If you have answered yes to one or more of these questions, you are probably using food as a way to anchor you — to give yourself a boundary where there is none. People describe this experience in a number of ways: "It is as if I have left my body and the food actually brings me back." "It's like I'm trying to find myself and there is food — my old friend. It feels safe." "If I don't diet, I can't contain the pain. Dieting helps me cope."

When we lose our definition, food is a point of reference. We know who we are in relationship to it. It bring us back to our physicality — a very real, tangible experience of ourselves.

Rigid Self-Definition — The "Super Trooper"

"Being with my mother, I begin to realize that I am existent for her, that my wishes and desires are sucked up into her, that what I have chosen to do has all been for her, really, in the end — that nothing has been left for me." (Journal, 1973)

Nelly's attempts at self-expression were bombarded by the constant scrutiny and stares of her mother. "I wasn't allowed to laugh, make noise, run or play. I was told who to play with, what to feel and how to think." Nelly developed a defensive exterior to keep her mother's intrusive energy out. She has trouble forming intimate relationships, prefers to live alone, and uses her obsession with food and weight to protect her from control by others. Nelly protects herself from feeling by her independence, ambition and rigid rules. She can't allow herself to feel her longings for closeness because closeness, to her, means invasion and injury.

Like Never Enoughers, Super Troopers were not supported in developing healthy Self-boundaries. Their true feelings and needs were not seen, heard or reflected, either. But because, as children, they felt powerless against the invasive style of their parents, they developed a rigid boundary which serves the dual function of cutting off their own needs and feelings (in order not to feel their fears) while protecting them from the dominating behavior of the parent.

Compulsive selves with Super Trooper tendencies tend to use food or body weight to keep others away. They may use food to isolate themselves or develop rigid rules that help them to feel safe. "It's okay to eat one half cup of rice but not one morsel more." This rigid way of thinking comes from the fear of being controlled by outside forces. "If I step outside my rules (let my guard down), the *food* will overwhelm me. I will be powerless to protect myself against it."

People with rigid self-definition need distance most of the time. They are comfortable being alone and tend toward isolation because, to them, intimacy means something will be taken from them. Their greatest fear is that of invasion because when people get too close, it reminds them of a childhood in which closeness meant abuse. When people get too close they fear the loss of definition and feel as if they are falling apart. Invasive or controlling parents do not hear the feelings of the child. For many children of such parents, feelings were discounted or crushed. The child's Self was inundated by the parent. Thus, when a Super Trooper comes close to feeling, she will experience the fear of being hurt.

Super Troopers use food, dieting, body weight (fat or thin) as a way to stay away from feelings and keep people away — to maintain some self-definition.

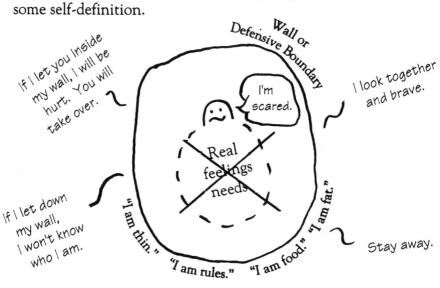

The Super Trooper

If you think you use food or weight to keep people away or if you have formed very rigid rules around your eating style, you are probably using food to guard against feelings, especially fear. Your issue is not so much the emptiness caused by lack of attention, but the sense of powerlessness caused by a controlling, manipulative or invasive parent.

Check this out by answering the following questions:
- Am I afraid of feeling?
- Do I have a hard time feeling?
- Do I prefer to be alone rather than with others?
- Do I prefer to have rules around eating rather than no rules?
- Do I compulsively need to be perfect at everything I do?
- Am I uncomfortable with anything that resembles losing control?
- Are my food binges triggered by people getting too close?
- Am I afraid of people using me?
- Do (or did) I have an abusive, controlling or manipulative parent?

If you have answered yes to any of the above questions, you probably have some Super Trooper characteristics. You may find it helpful to take some time to write about specific incidents.

Now, close your eyes and think of a time when you were a child and felt invaded in any way. Perhaps you were verbally, physically or sexually abused. Or, perhaps you didn't have space to explore your own feelings, thoughts and interests.

In whatever way you felt invaded, remember how this was for you.

Open your eyes and answer the following questions:
- How did I feel?
- What did I do with the feelings?
- Did I express them?
- Did I hold them back?
- How did I cope with invasion?
- Do I feel similarly today?
- How do I cope today?
- Does food play a part in my coping style?

Notice if at any time in recent months you have overeaten or restricted your food intake as a result of feeling manipulated, controlled or invaded. If you have, try to reconnect with the underlying feeling of powerlessness and ask yourself the following questions:
- Do I feel as if I am falling apart?
- Do I feel as if I can't function?
- Do I feel overwhelmed?
- Am I scared?
- Can I focus?
- Do I feel as if I am trying to swim in an ocean with no land in sight?

If you have answered yes to one or more of the above questions, you are probably using food as a way to anchor you, to give yourself a boundary where there is none.

As you can see, both the Never Enougher and the Super Trooper have a poorly formed sense of Self because of inaccurate mirroring, but the needs and emotional experience of each is very different.

The Never Enougher uses food to fill her longings and need for love. Her coping style is to attach to something (people, work, money, food) outside herself to feel safe. The underlying issue is "I won't exist without you." The greatest fear is that of abandonment ("If you leave me, I will fall apart.") The Super Trooper, by contrast, uses food and fat to protect herself from being controlled by others. Her coping style is control, rules and isolation. Playing the food game gives her a sense of power because the underlying issue is "I am powerless to be myself with you." Her greatest fear is that of invasion, "If I let you in, I won't exist. You will overpower me."

By now you probably have some idea as to whether you felt primarily abandoned or invaded as a child. In fact, most of us have felt both abandoned and invaded to varying degrees and therefore have both Never Enougher and Super Trooper characteristics. Certainly, if you were invaded, you were also abandoned, because when a child is told what to do or how to think or feel, her own desires, feelings and thoughts are not heard. She is also abandoned. Or, you may have had parents who were *both* absent *and* domineering.

Both of Tess's parents were alcoholic. Depending upon the situation, they were either working, out drinking or at home fighting. Tess never knew what to expect. Would they be there, or wouldn't they? If they were there, would they be unconscious or raging at her?

Don's dad was a controlling maniac. "He beat us kids for nothing at all. Where was my mother? She never stopped him. He was controlling; she was neglectful."

Rochelle's mom was frequently out doing volunteer work, or taking care of someone else's kids. "When I'd finally get some time with her, she'd want me to do things her way — clean my room, wear my pink dress (not my blue one), play with my dolls, not my paints (they were too messy). I never felt like I could be myself with her. I didn't know which was worse — having her with me, or not."

The combination of abandonment and invasion can exist in many ways in our families. Food may then be used to fill a longing *and* to push others away.

Let's see what happens when both abandonment and invasion are key elements in a child's life.

"Don't Go Too Far" and "Don't Get Too Close" — The "As Iffer"

"Saw Danny watching me today. Don't have time for him — so much to do. Aware of how I won't let myself love him. Will never be like mom, living for a man. Won't lose myself like her. Yet I fear his leaving me for someone else and so I flirt. So confused. Stay busy. Just stay busy." (Journal, 1974)

Elly longs for closeness yet fears being stifled, controlled or manipulated by the man she loves. Like most emotional eaters, Elly has both Never Enougher and Super Trooper characteristics.

While the Never Enougher feels defined and, therefore, safe *with people* and the Super Trooper feels defined and safe *when alone*, the As Iffer has no way to define herself. She can't let herself get close because closeness means being manipulated or controlled; yet, when alone, she longs for connection and love. One way to deal with this constant fear of losing oneself is to split off (separate) from the body. In fact, the way the As Iffer keeps from falling into the void is by thinking. Splitting off from her body is a sure way not to have the experience of Self-obliteration — but with it comes an inability to feel, to need, to know when she is hungry and when she is full. With no feelings or needs, there is no connection to Self at all. In fact, one of the characteristics of this type of person is to live an "idea" of who she is. "If I act *as if* I know who I am, I can fool myself and others." As Iffers are smart, intelligent, successful people who turn to food when a performance fails or when the ideas by which they live no longer prevent an awareness of their own emptiness. Because the As Iffer has no connection with her body-feelings, needs and values, when the ideas by which she lives no longer work, the whole of her life feels as if it is coming unglued. Hopefully, she will use this experience to push herself through the void to the center of herself. If not, she will seek solace in food.

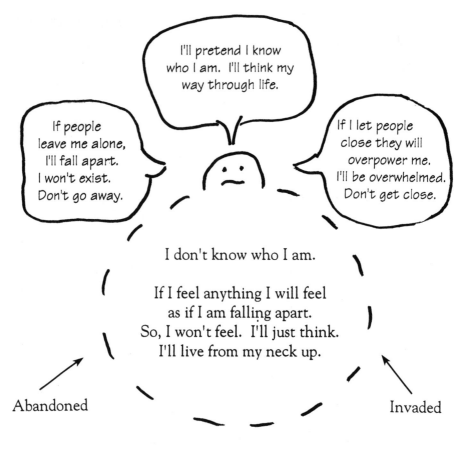

The As Iffer

If you feel pulled in two directions — if you need to be close to others, but are afraid of intimacy; if you push others away, then feel anxious because you are all alone — you probably have both abandonment and invasion issues. You use food to fill a longing and to keep others out. You live an idea or concept of what your life should be, but underneath, feel unfulfilled.

If you think this is true for you, go back and review the questions and exercises on pages 33-34 (Never Enougher) and pages 36-37 (Super Trooper). Notice if at any time in recent months you have overeaten or restricted as a result of either feeling abandoned or invaded. If you have, try to connect to the underlying feelings of emptiness and powerlessness. Answer the following questions:

- Do I feel as if I am falling apart?
- Do I feel as if I can't function?

- Do I feel overwhelmed?
- Am I scared?
- Can I focus?
- Do I feel as if I am trying to swim in an ocean with no land in sight?

If you have answered yes to one or more of the above questions, you are probably using food as a way to anchor you, to give yourself a boundary where there is none.

What Happens When Our Character Style Fails?

The "Never Enougher," "Super Trooper," and "As Iffer," are character styles that compulsive self creates in order to maintain a sense of definition despite the loss of a healthy Self-boundary.

Whenever a child is abandoned or invaded, the real Self (feelings, needs, interests) suffers an injury. The injury is experienced spiritually, emotionally and physically. Where there is injury, the organism learns to compensate for the missing part. When the part that is injured is our Self-image or boundary, we must either look outside ourselves for definition, or form rigid definitions.

We cannot function without some sort of boundary.
The experience of being without a boundary is unbearable and feels as if we are shattering into a multitude of tiny pieces.

When these styles fail us, we fall into the void and are thrown into an "identity crisis." All of a sudden we feel as if we are coming apart at the seams.

Anything can trigger this crisis. The only requirement is that it resemble the injury of our childhood. The Never Enougher who has clung to a dying relationship feels such a crisis when the relationship ends because it resembles the childhood abandonment experience of not being seen, heard or reflected. The Super Trooper may fall apart the morning she gains a few pounds, (or doesn't have time to exercise), because she is left with childhood feelings of powerlessness. The As Iffer may experience such a crisis when she realizes her life isn't working the way she thought it would — through aging, illness, loss of a job, or other critical events.

A good way to understand this "falling apart" experience is to take a look at the chart on the next page.

As you can see from this chart, when the character style and/or food game fails us, we fall back into the injury —the experience of being without a definition — that was caused by the abandoning or invasive behavior of our parents.

In the process of trying to lose weight or stop overeating, one must realize that the food game contains our identity.

**In the process of trying to eliminate the food game
(change one's weight, abstain from
emotional eating, stop dieting and so on),
the falling apart experience will probably occur.**

Remember that the compulsive self trait (the object to which the Never Enougher attaches, the rigid rules of Super Trooper, the ideas and achievements of the As Iffer, or playing the food game) *prevents* this experience of falling apart. It enables us to function by giving us a *semblance* of the "I'm okay" experience.

The Experience of the Fragmented Self[4]

Amy hangs up the phone. One of her important business clients has informed her that he's not going to continue using her services. She panics. "I can't move. I have five loads of dirty clothes that need to be laundered and I can't get myself together enough to do it." Although Amy was raised in affluence, as an infant she was given little true nurturing. Because of this, she doesn't trust her needs will be taken care of. When situations occur that threaten her safety, she responds as if she is that helpless infant all over again. Amy re-experiences her childhood fears of abandonment — her heart beats faster, her head spins, the pressure in her chest increases and she loses her ability to function in her adult world. Amy falls apart.

Esther's husband wants sex. She doesn't. Although she has the power to simply say "No," childhood incest issues recreate feelings of

---

[4]Fragmentation model and "Steps Out of Fragmentation" are taken from *Body, Self and Soul* and IBP training. They are adapted here for emotional eaters.

Injury: Abandonment and Invasion

Fear: Abandonment: "If you leave me, I won't exist." Invasion: "If I let you in, I won't exist."

Coping Style: Rises up out of the body into the head ("mentalizes"). Splits off into abstractions, concepts and fantasies. Spaces out.

Boundary: Can be either no boundary or rigid boundary.

Feelings: Not in touch with them because not in the body.

Food Game: Used to numb feelings and needs, fill an underlying emptiness and to isolate.

Underlying Issue: Emptiness and powerlessness.

Character Style: Super Trooper

Injury: Invasion.

Fear: Invasion. "If I let you in, I won't exist. You will over-power me."

Coping Style: Isolates. Rigid Rules. Need for excessive control to feel safe.

Boundary: Defended and rigid. Excessively fat or thin.

Feelings: Buried.

Food Game: Controlled and rigid. Gives sense of power. Used to isolate. Numbs anxiety when others try to get too close.

Underlying Issue: Powerlessness.

Character Style: Never Enougher

Injury: Abandonment.

Fear: Abandonment "If you leave me, I won't exist."

Coping Style: Attaches to people or other outside objects in order to feel safe.

Boundary: None.

Feelings: Longing. Neediness. Emptiness.

Food Game: Numbs feelings and needs in order to maintain relationship. Fills emptiness and longings. Numbs anxiety felt when others try to separate.

Underlying Issue: Emptiness.

Food Game and Character Style Protect from Injury

Abandonment — Neglect, Insufficient Limits — "I don't exist"

Invasion — Abuse, Control, Manipulation — "I am Powerless"

SELF — Body, Feelings, Needs

Injury — Guilt, Fear, Shame

helplessness which cause Esther to first comply, then fly into a rage. She loses her ability to deal with her husband rationally.

Whenever Susie feels judged or criticized, she disintegrates. "As a kid I was yelled at all the time. I couldn't do anything right. When playing, I was too noisy. When quietly reading, I'd be told to do my homework. When doing homework, I was criticized for not helping with the chores. Why couldn't they accept what I was doing?" Susie's greatest unmet need is for approval. When she doesn't get it from the people in her life, she is overcome with intense feelings of shame and rage.

The word used to describe the experiences of Amy, Esther and Susie is "fragmentation." Fragmentation is an out-of-control experience of falling apart, self-obliteration, or disintegration, in which we have no Self-definition or Self-boundary.

One workshop participant drew a picture of her fragmentation:

"The Eater" by Lindly Otte
(used with permission)

Another describes her fragmentation as "free falling in a dark abyss." Yet another describes it as "being paralyzed, like an animal, by headlights at night." Some of the symptoms of fragmentation are powerlessness, despair, emptiness, rage, abusive behavior, and feelings of extreme guilt, fear and shame that interfere with functioning.

The food game enables us to avoid the experience of fragmentation.

For example, when the person or thing the Never Enougher has attached to fails her, she will cling to food in a desperate attempt to prevent the fragmentation from occurring. Many Never Enoughers live in an ongoing attachment/fragmentation cycle that looks something like this:

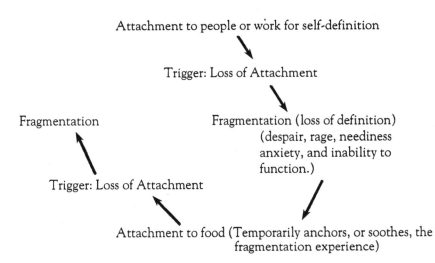

Periods of sanity marked by attachments are interspersed between periods of fragmentation. The Never Enougher feels secure that she is loved or, is doing well at work, or is making lots of money, and then something happens — her boyfriend is unavailable, her boss is unhappy with her last report, income slackens — and her anxiety level soars. Feelings of shame and fear overwhelm her ability to function.

In order to regain her equilibrium, she may overeat, in an attempt not to feel the uncomfortable feelings and to gain some sense of control by attaching, once again, to an object that temporarily anchors her. Once she feels "put back together again," she will be able to cope temporarily with her boyfriend's unavailability (*"Oh well, maybe he's out with a friend"*) or her boss's unhappiness (*"He's been irritable a lot lately. Maybe it has nothing to do with me."*) or her decreased income (*"Next month I'll work harder and make it up."*). While food has enabled her to cope temporarily with these issues, she has not done the work necessary to understand the cause of fragmentation and heal it. So, when her boyfriend is again unavailable, her boss unhappy, or her income decreases, she will fragment and turn to food again. Food rarely exists as an attachment object in and of itself. It most always is preceded by another object that has failed.

When the defensive or rigid boundary style of the Super Trooper fails, she will cling to food in an attempt to prevent fragmentation. Super Troopers live in an ongoing isolation/fragmentation cycle that looks like this.

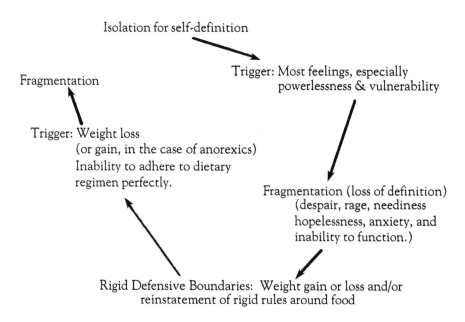

Isolation for self-definition

Fragmentation

Trigger: Most feelings, especially
    powerlessness & vulnerability

Trigger: Weight loss
    (or gain, in the case of anorexics)
    Inability to adhere to dietary
    regimen perfectly.

Fragmentation (loss of definition)
    (despair, rage, neediness
    hopelessness, anxiety, and
    inability to function.)

Rigid Defensive Boundaries: Weight gain or loss and/or
reinstatement of rigid rules around food

When a Super Trooper becomes threatened by feelings, especially powerlessness and vulnerability, or by what she perceives as too

much outside control, she may panic. In an attempt to avoid the fragmentation, she will overeat in order to gain weight and/or implement
rigid rules around food and diet.

When excessive weight is used to maintain isolation, weight loss
can cause fragmentation.[6] Loss of weight creates a vulnerability
which may trigger out-of-control eating episodes in an unconscious
attempt to regain the lost weight and feel protected again. When not
overeating, many Super Troopers maintain strict dietary controls.
When they break their diet, they may experience such shame and
hopelessness (fragmentation) that they resume out-of-control eating
in an unconscious attempt to avoid the feelings. Excessive body
weight, dietary regimens *and* out-of-control eating are attempts to
avoid powerlessness, vulnerability and other feelings. When these
feelings are experienced, fragmentation can occur.

Defining Your Fragmentation

Common symptoms of fragmentation include feelings of powerlessness, despair, emptiness, rage and extreme guilt, fear and shame.
The way we experience fragmentation in the body varies from
individual to individual. People report an inability to focus, pounding
in the chest, constriction in the jaw, neck, chest or stomach, tingling
of hands and feet, headaches, nausea, loss of equilibrium, tightness of
muscles, tears, etc. Many overeaters describe a nervousness, an
ungroundedness, an inability to feel as if they are present in their
bodies. One workshop participant told me outright, "I feel as if I leave
my body." Another woman describes her bingeing as "trying to feel
grounded, trying to come back out of the spinning sensations in my
head." I've even had reports of hearing sounds and seeing colors.

To help identify your fragmentation, you must first define your
personal symptoms and sensations. You may do this now by remembering how you feel before overeating. Write the fragmentation
symptom (eg., "I feel powerless and panicky") and the body sensations (eg., "My insides are exploding; can't sit still; skin is crawling")
that accompany these feelings. If this is too difficult to remember,

---

[6]Likewise, when excessive thinness is used to maintain isolation, weight gain or the
fear of weight gain can cause fragmentation.

write the symptoms and sensations of fragmentation in your journal *before* you overeat. You may have to resist eating longer than you normally would in order to get the feelings! (More about this on page 57.)

CHAPTER FOUR

Repairing The Injury

FRAGMENTATION HAPPENS WHEN THE SELF DOES NOT HAVE AN IDENTITY. IT IS AS IF THE INDIVIDUAL IS A MASS OF UNFORMED ENERGY. THERE IS NOTHING IN ITSELF WRONG WITH UNFORMED ENERGY, BUT UNFORMED ENERGY CANNOT FUNCTION IN THE WORLD. THERE MUST BE A CONTAINER. WHEN THERE IS A WEAK IDENTITY, THE FOOD GAME HOLDS THE INDIVIDUAL'S ENERGY SO THAT SHE IS ABLE TO FUNCTION. WHEN YOU TAKE THE FOOD GAME AWAY, IT IS VERY IMPORTANT THAT THE INDIVIDUAL HAVE A REPLACEMENT FOR IT. THE NEW CONTAINER (IDENTITY) MUST EVOLVE FROM A CHANGE IN SELF-PERCEPTION. THAT IS WHY FULL HEALING REQUIRES MANY YEARS OF TRANSFORMATIONAL WORK. THE PERSON MUST, IN FACT, REBUILD HER SELF-IMAGE. ONE WAY THAT THIS MAY BE ACCOMPLISHED IS THROUGH ONE'S CONNECTION TO AN OBJECT THAT WILL BECOME THE PERSON'S "GOOD PARENT": A 12-STEP PROGRAM, A HIGHER POWER, A THERAPIST OR TREATMENT PROGRAM. CONNECTING WITH A NURTURING PROGRAM OR PERSON THAT HELPS TO BUILD HEALTHY BOUNDARIES IS AN APPROPRIATE WAY FOR THE INDIVIDUAL WHO IS WITHOUT AN IDENTITY TO BUILD ONE.

I am left alone and hungry. I cry out, but nobody comes. I panic. I cry louder. Nobody comes. To me, minutes seem like years, and still nobody comes. I am alone and afraid. Only I can't name the fear and I can't say to myself "someone will come" because I don't have words. I exist in the ever present, infinite sensation of infancy.

When Amy was seven months old, the only way she knew to ask for holding was by crying. If she didn't get what she needed, a vague something didn't feel comfortable. She cried louder. If she still didn't get it, she panicked. Then, Amy did the only thing she could do to protect herself, she depressed her breathing as a way to numb the panicky feeling.[1]

On her own now, with responsibility for herself and her children, old insecurities are easily re-experienced. When Amy's business suffers a loss, her body remembers how it was to need and not get. She panics just like she did when she was seven months old.

As first, Amy has no understanding of what is happening. As she applies herself to healing the fragmentation, she begins to sense how it was for her as an infant. The falling apart experience is, in fact, the same panic she experienced then.

When fragmented, the overwhelming need is to feel put back together again. The way many of us try to get this "I'm okay" experience is by playing the food game. But, as I have shown, this is only a temporary solution and becomes less and less reliable as time goes by. In fact, even winning the food game *cannot* give us the *real* sense of well-being we are after because the game is based on a false structure. True well-being can only arise from repairing the original injury and reclaiming the Self.

Once you are committed to heal — to move inward toward the center of Self, rather than back outward to the periphery of compulsive self — there are specific things you can do to accomplish this.

---

[1]Like Amy, many of us learn to constrict the breathing process, to build up defensive holding patterns in the very musculature of the abdomen and chest, in order not to feel the pain of our injuries. But, in so doing, we stop the alive feelings as well. IBP therapy uses breathing and stress release techniques to unlock these blocks, enabling us to experience a greater degree of aliveness and well-being.

Because the fragmented state is an experiential repeat of the childhood injury, we can use it to give ourselves what we didn't know how to ask for as children.

Because Amy is now an adult with adult resources, she can give the infant within her what she couldn't get then. She can become her own "Good Parent," so to speak — to see, hear and reflect to her inner child her real feelings and needs, to give her the nurturing and verbal messages she desperately longs for. Remember, the crucial issue underlying the out-of-control experience is the loss of Self-definition. It is the mirroring (listening, acknowledging, validating and responding) that is crucial for Amy's healing because the mirroring will give that infant inside her a sense of safety, containment and validation, which, in turn will provide the Self-boundary she never got.

Pulling Out of Fragmentation — Mirroring Your Inner Child

We carry the memory of our childhood (both positive and negative) within us. These memories affect our perceptions and thinking processes, our feelings and body stance. Because our childhood experience has greatly affected the way our adult self operates in the world, the process of reconnecting to these experiences with adult awareness can enable us to change our adult way of responding to the present day events in our lives. This is called inner child healing.

Fragmentation results when a situation in our present life resembles a childhood situation in which we felt either abandoned or invaded. When this happened as a child, we were not able to see an accurate reflection of our Self. We formed an image of ourselves that either was distorted ("I am bad," or "I am sad," when I'm really angry) or non-existent ("I don't exist," "I don't matter.")

Each time a situation resembles the original injury, we fall back into the distortion and negative self-talk, losing whatever positive self-image we do have or have constructed. We fall back again and again, until we recognize the injury and give ourselves (the child within us) the actual reflection it needs.

To do this, it is important to stop trying to pretend we are okay. We may strive to "keep it together" with a forced smile, or by trying to do things perfectly all of the time, or by covering up unresolved issues with affirmations, and so on. While these are socially admirable adult traits, they do not serve the child within us. What you needed most as a child was to be heard. The longer you put off hearing your own child within, the longer you perpetuate the wound and the greater it becomes.

The injury to the child is two-fold. First, the injury is one of *not being heard*, per se. It is an injury to the Self. This injury is healed by simply listening, acknowledging and validating. In this way, the child begins to experience and believe her own feelings and needs. She comes to know her feelings and needs are separate, as good as and equal to that of the adult (in this case, you). Your wounded child begins to form an appropriate boundary. Second, the injury results from the *unmet need* within the child. This need can be for any number of things. It can be a need for recognition (which you are already addressing by simply listening to your child) or the need for safety, trust, support, confidence, feeling special, setting limits, feeling sexual or being different.

Knowing how to heal this injury comes from listening. What the child within you needs will be communicated to you by your "child." You can then respond to her need — supply her with the missing piece. You can give her (you) what you never got from your parents. Doing this will enable your child to feel put back together again and heal the fragmentation.

The method I most highly recommend for both listening and responding to your child is journal writing.[2] Of course, a good therapist who is trained in helping you heal your childhood traumas (being careful not to perpetuate or re-injure them) and who can help you get yourself out of fragmentation is an invaluable asset, but ultimately, you must eventually learn to do this yourself because our therapists (or anyone else for that matter) cannot be available to us whenever we need them. In fact, becoming dependent on a therapist

---

[2]If you are unfamiliar with the methods of journal writing, there are some excellent books on this subject. See Resources pp. 123-124.

to do this for us, while temporarily helpful, may later only *perpetuate* the "attachment" needs of the Never Enougher characteristics within us rather than heal them.

Forming Self-Boundaries — Dialoging with your Inner Child

Dialoging is a journal writing process in which you are conversing with a part of yourself, just as you would with another person. The goal is to access a deeper layer of information than would normally be available in one's everyday consciousness. This is done by first relaxing. You ask that part of yourself to express itself, to tell you what it is feeling and why. You listen non-judgmentally. When it is through saying what it wishes to say, you respond from your other part.

Example:

Bob: *Why are you bingeing?*
Child: *I'm angry at you.*
Bob: *Why?*
Child: *Because you don't listen to me.*

You can begin this process by simply closing your eyes and remembering what it felt like to be a kid.[3] You may remember a specific incident or a series of incidents or you may have vague sensations or feelings.

Then, simply ask your child questions: Who is your best friend? What is your favorite thing to do? How do you feel? Is there anything you'd like to say to me? What do you need right now?

Write your child's responses in your journal. Write quickly so you do not have time to judge what she is saying (or you may write from her perspective with your non-dominant hand).[4] You can respond whenever it feels appropriate to do so. Write back and forth,

---

[3]If you have been diagnosed with any form of dissociative or traumatic disorder or if the memories are too discomforting, I recommend you do not do inner child work or any dialoging without first consulting your therapist.

[4]See Lucia Capacchione, Ph.D. *Recovery of Your Inner Child* (New York: Simon & Schuster, 1991). Shows you how to have a firsthand experience of your inner child by writing and drawing with your non-dominant hand.

first from your child's perspective and then from yours, until the process feels complete. Then ask, What did I learn about myself? About my child? How am I feeling right now?

Practice dialoging with your child *before* you fragment so that when you fall apart, you will already have had some experience. Trying to dialogue with your child for the first time when fragmented may be like trying to learn a new language while swimming in the middle of the ocean, with no land in sight on a stormy day!

Dialogue often. The more you do, the more your child will feel heard, and the stronger her Self-boundary will become.[5]

Determining Your Child's Injury — The Binge Journal

Now that you are listening to your child, allowing her to express her feelings and needs to you — you will hear her injury. Does she feel neglected? Is she scared of being used by others? Is she afraid of being rejected or left alone? Is she afraid of being controlled or sexually invaded?

Locating your child's injury is the second step in the process of healing fragmentation. If you didn't get what you needed as a child, you learned to suppress your needs. This is the same as saying you suppressed your Self. If we don't know what we need, we don't know our Self. Every fragmentation experience is a replay of a time in which a need was unfulfilled and was therefore suppressed. That is why, when we fragment, it feels as if we lose our Self. We do! No awareness of need, no Self. Needs must be acknowledged or they die. So, the second part of healing is *determining* the need, *acknowledging* the need, then whenever possible, *fulfilling* the need.

I ask all my clients and workshop participants to keep a Binge Journal. A Binge Journal is a separate section of your Journal devoted to understanding and writing about your patterns of emotional

---

[5]If you have trouble connecting with your inner child, there are a number of books and audiotapes published to assist this process. See Resources, pp. 123-124. Another option would be to connect with a therapist in your area who is trained in inner child work.

eating. It will enable you to locate the situations that have triggered your emotional eating in order to determine the underlying need of your inner child so that you can respond to that need. When a person comes into a private session and tells me he or she binged last night and has no idea why, I ask her to review the hours preceding the binge, paying special attention to situations and people that might have caused discomfort. It is always possible to connect emotional eating to a specific person, situation or series of events.

You can do this yourself before or after you overeat or binge. Sit down, close your eyes, and take a few deep belly breaths to help you relax. Remember the last time you overate or binged. Retrace your steps backward from the moment you put that first compulsive bite into your mouth, as if you are slowly rewinding a film of your day. You may have to go back a few days. How were you feeling that morning? Then, retrace your steps forward slowly, *staying with your feelings*. (It is very important to stay with your feelings.) What happened next? Did anything make you uncomfortable? If not, keep moving forward until you locate the event that caused some kind of discomfort. Then answer the following questions in your Binge Journal:

- Describe the situation that triggered emotional eating or desire to overeat.
- Who was involved?
- What about this incident made me uncomfortable?
- What was I feeling? (Look for feelings of rejection, power-lessness, restlessness, anxiety, fear, anger, hurt, etc.)
- Was I afraid of losing someone's love or approval?
- Was I afraid of being used or manipulated?
- Is there anything about this situation or my feelings that resemble my childhood in anyway? If yes, describe.
- What did my child need from a parent that she didn't get?

Dialogue with your child around her issues. Let her express her feelings to you. Let her express her needs. If you can fulfill her needs, then let her know this and do it. If you cannot, be honest with her, but let her know that you will continue to listen to her and will do your best to help her. After working with your child, come back to the situation that triggered emotional eating.

Answer the following questions:
- Does this feel resolved?
- Are my needs being met?
- What might I do to meet my needs?
- What might I do to resolve the situation?

Steve shared his experiences with using the Binge Journal in group.

"I had gone to the store for some groceries for my girlfriend, Julie. When I returned, the door to her house was locked and she was gone. I didn't have her key and so I was forced to either wait outside in the car or go back to my house. I didn't want to go home. I was furious. I immediately felt like someone had punched me in the chest. I knew I was fragmenting because I lost my reality. My mind kept telling me that there must have been a miscommunication, but it didn't help. I felt as if I was bursting at the seams and I wanted to rip open the box of pretzels I had bought for that evening. Then, I remembered the Binge Journal. I started writing. My inner child came forward immediately. I sobbed. It was intense. I remembered when Mother died, how alone and scared I felt. Somehow I was able to connect the feelings I was having to my mother's death and the need to eat the pretzels disappeared. It was profound. When Julie returned, we talked about it. It was a misunderstanding. Now, I'm grateful for the misunderstanding because it enabled me to reconnect with the loss of my mother and to understand how that loss affects my relationship to food today."

Most emotional eating is preceded by fragmentation states similar to the one described by Steve. Situations that trigger emotional eating most always remind us of the ways in which we either felt abandoned or invaded as children. These ways need not be as dramatic as the death of a parent, but may have the same emotional effect, nevertheless. For example, I had one client who always overate when she got home from work. Experimenting with not eating brought up feelings of boredom and unrest. "I have to eat to relax. If not, my skin begins to crawl," she explained. As we talked further I discovered her love of music. "Why don't you play your piano instead of eating?" I asked. "Because I have to do it perfectly or not at all!" Further probing revealed a childhood in which "doing it right" was more important than having fun. Entrapped by her intolerance of imperfection, she cuts herself off from the pleasure her creativity could bring. Eating is a good way not to have to feel the boredom or the anxiety generated by fear of her parents' rejection.

I ask most clients to refrain from emotional eating as long as possible in order to feel the fragmentation — the panic, fear, shame, rage, anxiety and whatever physical sensations accompany those feelings. This is especially true if you are one of those people who overeats all the time. Then, the only way to connect with fragmentation is to *not* eat for a specific period of time — an afternoon or evening, or perhaps a greater part of the day. Stay with your feelings. Ask yourself, am I bored, anxious, nervous, panicky? Is there anything scary or uncomfortable about my feelings? If yes, what? How do my feelings connect with childhood fears of abandonment or invasion? As you allow yourself to feel the fragmentation and bring yourself through it without food, you will begin to live beyond the food game.

Good Parent Messages[6]

To help heal your childhood injuries, I have included a list of "Good Parent" messages that are typically absent from many families. In order for the child to develop a strong Self, these messages must have been implied within the context of your parent's verbal statements. Some or all of these Good Parent messages may have been missing from your childhood or they may have been spoken but not meant. For example, many parents tell their children, "I love you," yet the child grows up feeling unloved. A child needs to *feel* the parent's love. This is done through time and attention given, eye contact, touch and tone of voice. When a parent says to a child in an authoritarian tone of voice, "No TV until your homework is done,"

---

[6] The specific "Good Parent Messages" are from *Body, Self and Soul: Sustaining Integration* and are reprinted with permission of Humanics Limited, Atlanta.

the implied message is, "You are not mature or capable enough to make your own decisions, so I will do it for you." The missing Good Parent message would be, "I have confidence in you. I am sure you can do it."

It is your job, as an adult, to help your inner child receive the messages she never got. Take some time to review the following messages. Notice which messages feel strange, foreign or stand out in some way. These will probably be the messages you will need to add to your Binge Journal for healing your fragmentation.

_____ I want you.
_____ I love you.
_____ I'll take care of you.
_____ You can trust me.
_____ I'll be there for you.
_____ It is not what you do but who you are that I love.
_____ You are special to me.
_____ I love you, and I give you permission to be different from me.
_____ Sometimes I will tell you "no" and that's because I love you.
_____ My love will make you well.
_____ I see you and I hear you.
_____ You can trust your inner voice.
_____ I have confidence in you. I am sure you can do it.
_____ I will set limits and I will enforce them.
_____ If you fall down, I will pick you up.
_____ You are special to me. I am proud of you.
_____ I give you permission to make mistakes.
_____ I give you permission to be a sexual being.
_____ I give you permission to be the same as I am AND more than I am AND less than I am.

Amy shared her use of the Good Parent messages in group. *"When my business suffers a loss, the child within me feels alone and scared. No one is there to take care of her. I clearly identified the following* missing messages: 'I'll take care of you,' 'I'll be there for you,' and 'You don't have to be afraid anymore.'" Because Amy has identified the fear as a childhood fear, her adult Self can be the Good Parent to her child — giving her child the message she never got. "*I find that writing the messages over and over again in my journal really helps. Sometimes I clutch my doll or pillow while saying the words as if rocking myself to sleep. My breathing eases and my body relaxes.*"

Sandra shared this: "*At the doctor's last week, I bled heavily. The doctor seemed worried. I was scared. I became agitated and overwhelmed. I remembered that as a child I was frequently left alone when sick. Both my parents had to work, so they couldn't be with me. I tried to be brave, but inside I really hurt. The messages that feel good to me are 'My love will make you well,' 'You are special to me' and 'I'll be there for you.'*"

Henry shared his experiences, too. "*As a child I felt responsible for my mother. My dad died when I was eight years old, so I became the man of the house early. My mother and sister depended on me and I felt I had to meet their expectations. Today, when I make mistakes or let someone down I feel real bad. Yesterday, my boss asked me to complete a report in half the time previously expected. I knew I couldn't do it, but I told him 'yes.' Since then, I've been unable to concentrate or focus on anything. The messages that seem to help me most are 'It's not what you do, but who you are that I love' and 'I give you permission to make mistakes.'*"

It is now your turn to identify the messages missing from your childhood. Check the ones you think may have been missing. Feel free to adjust them to fit your own situation more accurately. Look at the messages you've checked and compare them to your Binge Journal. Which messages tend to be lacking from situations that trigger emotional eating?

You may want to post these messages on your refrigerator. Then, when you begin to fragment or want to overeat, you will be reminded of them. You can begin saying them to yourself immediately, write them in your journal and/or use the "Steps Out of Fragmentation" which follows.

Steps Out of Fragmentation Using the Binge Journal

> *Humpty Dumpty sat on a wall.*
> *Humpty Dumpty had a great fall.*
> *All the king's horses and all the king's men*
> *Couldn't put Humpty together again.*

When you fall apart, think of Humpty Dumpty. Sitting on the wall he is whole and together. The fallen Humpty is fragmented. Try to imagine Humpty doing anything at all from his shattered condition. Impossible. When you are fragmented, the first order of business is to get glued back together — hopefully in a way that supports your moving inward into the center of your Self.

The following steps are designed to get you out of fragmentation by helping you locate the childhood injury directly related to the events leading up to the emotional eating (which is covering up the fragmentation) so that you can mirror your child accurately and give your child the messages that were missing from your childhood. These messages are the missing puzzle pieces. By picking them up and inserting them in their proper place, a whole picture of your Self will begin to emerge. You can then come back to the present and respond to the trigger event in a way that fulfills your needs and accurately reflects your whole Self (rather than your compulsive self).

I suggest doing these steps before you overeat or binge. This will enable you to heal faster. However, if that's too difficult (which it may be at first), then do them afterwards. (As mentioned, if you overeat frequently, rather than binge, you may *have to* refrain from overeating to experience the fragmentation.)

1. Remember Humpty and DO NOT try to be functional — DO NOT try to relate to people or to accomplish anything. Your only job is to tend to yourself.
2. Acknowledge that the feelings are triggered by old childhood injuries. DO NOT use these feelings as a basis for making present day "adult" decisions, or as a basis for creating "adult" relationships.

3. Know that this condition is temporary. It is not a reflection of who you are for all time. You will put yourself back together again and you will feel good again.

4. Give yourself permission to be alone in order to feel and explore what you are feeling.

5. Close your eyes. Take five deep, long breaths into your lower abdomen. Relax. Whether you have overeaten or not, think about the event or series of events that have triggered the onset of your desire to eat. Retrace your steps backward, as if you are slowly rewinding a film of your day. You may have to go back a few days. How were you feeling that morning? Then, retrace your steps forward slowly, *staying with your feelings.* What happened next? Did anything make you uncomfortable? If not, continue to move forward until you locate the event that caused some kind of discomfort.

6. Open your eyes and write in your Binge Journal. Answer the following questions:
    *   What about this incident made me uncomfortable?
    *   What was I feeling? (Look for feelings of rejection, powerlessness, restlessness, anxiety, fear, anger, hurt, etc.)
    *   Was I afraid of losing someone's love or approval? Was I afraid of being used or manipulated?
    *   Did I fragment? If yes, describe how you know you were fragmenting. List the symptoms and the body sensations.
    *   Is there anything about this situation, or my feelings, that resemble my childhood in anyway? If yes, describe.
    *   What did my child need from a parent that she didn't get?
    *   What do I need right now?

7. Dialogue with your inner child.

8. Visualize your child and yourself receiving what you need.

9. Write the appropriate "Good Parent Message" that was missing from your childhood at least 20 times in your journal.

   The most important aspect of repeating these messages is to have an *experience* of them. It may be helpful to remember a time when you actually *felt* what the message is communicating. Perhaps this feeling was obtained through an interaction with a relative, friend or pet. Or, perhaps you yourself gave this message to another.

   Some people have difficulty finding an experience to relate to. If this is true for you, seek out and observe people whom you believe embody these messages. Spend time with them and allow them to give you what you are missing. Continue to write or say the messages to yourself at the same time. Eventually you will have an experience of their meaning.

10. Come back to the situation that has triggered or might have triggered emotional eating. Answer the following questions: Does this feel resolved? Are my needs being met? If not, what might I do to meet my needs? What might I do to resolve the situation?

11. Bring yourself back into the present. You can do this by looking around the room, naming objects and colors. Feel the space your body occupies as it rests upon your chair.

Once you have located the injury through recognition of the trigger event and its similarity to your childhood, have given your wounded inner child what was missing from her childhood, and have repositioned yourself in the present, you will probably feel put back together again. If you do not, continue to take time out for yourself. You may want to try working with a supportive person who is willing to help you connect with your feelings and explore this issue further.

After doing the Steps Out of Fragmentation a number of times, you will begin to see a pattern. When this happens, you may be able to shorten the process. Knowing the patterns may enable you to recognize the fragmentation symptoms, their trigger events and childhood injuries immediately. You will then be able to stop the fragmentation by going straight to the Good Parent Message.

About a week after the completion of a weekend workshop, Rachel shared this with me privately: *"When I left your workshop I went to the store. There was a guy that was very attractive to me. My head began to spin and I felt as if the insides of my stomach were exploding. I knew I was fragmenting. In the past I would have eaten a whole box of chocolate chip cookies. Instead, I used the Steps Out of Fragmentation. The feeling underneath my craving was longing. I wanted to be in relationship with this guy and felt as if this could never happen. I remembered feeling stupid and ugly as a child, Daddy telling me I'd never be any good to anyone. I realized immediately that I had internalized his message.*

"This handsome man was a symbol of everything the child in me couldn't have. In my mind, I searched for the missing messages. I told myself, I could and would have a relationship. I kept saying to myself, 'I give you permission to love and be loved. I give you permission to be a sexual being.' The effect was immediate. My head stopped spinning. My chest calmed down and the most amazing thing was, I left the store without the cookies."

CHAPTER FIVE

Your Healing Power

SOMETHING ENLIVENS THE PHYSICAL ORGAN-
ISM. SOMETHING DIFFERENTIATES LIVING FROM
NON-LIVING MATTER. CALL IT WHAT YOU WILL
— AN ENERGY, A FORCE, GOD, SPIRIT — BUT
KNOW THAT THIS POWER IS THE VERY SOURCE
OF LIFE AND, WHEN WE ALIGN WITH IT, HAS THE
POWER TO HEAL.

The room is filled with women — some very heavy, others slim, distant. I feel far away. Each one in turn stands up and says, "My name is _____. I'm a compulsive eater," and shares a story, or a feeling . They all listen. No one responds. I listen in wonder and then try the words on for size, "My name is Jane. I'm a compulsive eater."

A little voice in me rebels. I say it again because they tell me I have to admit to it, remember it always, if I want to be free. "Admit to your powerlessness. Never forget you are a compulsive eater!"

"You are a compulsive eater. You are a compulsive eater!"

Those words echo through my mind. "I am a compulsive eater," I think, trying to drown out the little rebellious voice.

I obey them in my ignorance, temporarily choosing to stay identified with the compulsive eater that cries out for attention. Yet the voice within me will not be squelched.

"You are not a compulsive eater. You are greater than that. Come find me. Be with me. Never again will you need to overeat." I feel this voice within me, now silently appearing, then drifting away, only to reappear again and again. Most often the loud roar of compulsive self drowns her out. But she is there, ever so quiet, yet persistent.

I try to hold onto her. I try to keep her with me. When she fades, I search for her. I think, "If I could only make her real, make her stay, then I will be released forever from this private Hell."

F or years I searched to find the power behind the little voice that said, "You are not a compulsive eater. You are greater than that." The misery of my shattered life propelled me forward.

"Last night I ate like a fiend and had sweaty anxious dreams over the performance — things going wrong, insecurities. I am very intense and anxious this morning and fat. Well, at least I know it's fear of not being able to pull this thing off and there is no real reason not to if I keep a cool head and meditate every day." (Journal, 1974)

For nine years, I would not leave the house until I had meditated for at least an hour every morning. Looking back, I now understand that meditating was my anchor. It was the island that promised survival in the vast ocean of my fragmented being. At that time in my life I was always in a state of fragmentation. I was lost and scared. And it was this promise — of a greater power within me — that enabled me to survive.

Rigorously, daily, I practiced my meditation. I bathed myself for one hour daily in the light of love. Then, I would leave my house, go to work and fall apart. But, I knew that I always had the light to return to.

Four years into my recovery, I became aware of a female force within me, a kind of great Mother who possessed awesome abilities to love and forgive. And I came to realize that when I called upon her, at any time of day or night, I was able to feel loved and nurtured. I no longer needed to wait for my morning meditation to center myself. Instantly the shame, guilt and fear disappeared. With her love I felt whole, could trust myself and move on.

The child, by nature, is powerless. It needs a greater power outside itself — its parent — to feel safe, cared for and defined. Fragmented, we need the same thing.

As adults we can get this care from a greater power, as well. The form this power takes will be yours alone to determine. For some, it is the Good Parent, for others, it is God or their higher self, the Goddess, or an undefinable force or energy. However we *think* of this power, it is always accompanied by a mysterious healing energy. As we consciously seek to align our psyche with this power, the shattered pieces of our fragmented self re-emerge whole

I have worked with many people. Some believe in a higher power and some do not. But I have found that no matter how skeptical the person, a connection with this healing power can occur, and when it does, healing *always* takes place.

If you have a strong spiritual belief, use it to heal yourself. If you do not, look for this power within the reaches of your own Self — the power to love, to connect with your own innate wisdom or to feel profound peace.

One client of mine is adamantly agnostic. She refuses to believe in a higher power outside herself. Yet, she has found this higher power within as an expanded and open condition of her own physical self. "I know I am in my higher power when I feel relaxed, open, alive and centered."

Another client of mine, emotionally and spiritually abused by a punitive religious belief system, was shamed to her core by parents who believed in the original sin of mankind. To this day she cannot rid herself of the fear of God's wrath and the deep-seated belief in her own wickedness. Every mistake she makes throws her into a fragmented experience of shame — a darkness that is very difficult to climb out of.

Because of her religious associations, it is impossible to work with her from a straightforward spiritual perspective. Yet, this woman is highly capable of reaching into the depths of her Self and connecting with the healing energy. Her Wise Self is everything her "God" was not. She is loving, nurturing and compassionate. In Her presence, shame doesn't stand a chance.

Ellen is a strikingly beautiful young woman with red hair, tan skin and a strong body. At our first session, I ask her why she is seeking help.

"When I look in the mirror, I see an unattractive, overweight woman. I'm lost. If I diet and try to lose weight, I'm back into bingeing and purging. I want to know what I really look like. My friends tell me I'm not fat. I have no idea. I can't tell."

In our second session Ellen and I explore this distortion further. I have her close her eyes and visualize a source of light above the top of her head, opening and releasing a shower of light down through her body. This visualization of light helps Ellen to connect with the nurturing energy of her healing power.

As we focus the light throughout her body, Ellen *observes* her body's reaction.

"There is pain in my stomach and it is dark. The light won't move in there." She is crying. "There is too much pain in there. My stomach feels big and fat and there is a lot of shame and badness."

Without establishing a connection with the healing power, reaching deeply into shame can propel us further into addiction. Focusing on the pain without first making a commitment to heal the pain, would be like reopening a wound. What's the point? The wound is exposed. It hurts. If the healing energy is weak there may be little or no healing. But, if the healing energy is strong, and if we know how to direct that energy into the wound, then we can safely re-enter the wound in order to make the proper preparations for its healing.[1]

Light is a universal symbol of healing and is used by many cultures to amplify the healing power. It is not necessary to "see" the light, only to experience its effects. You may feel calm, relaxed, warm or safe. Or, you may become aware of darkness. In much the same way as a candle illuminates the cobwebs hidden in the dark corners of a basement, light reveals the tangle of repressed thoughts, feelings and self-perceptions.

Imagine that you can take a trip into this basement of your psyche. Here all about you, but hidden from sight, are the cobwebs of your conditioning. You do not need them and you do not want them anymore, but they hang around because you can't see them. You want them out because they are making your life miserable, but you can't get to them because it's just too dark to see.

Then someone hands you a candle. You see a hazy form right under your nose. You bring the candlelight closer, becoming aware of

---

[1] For a more complete description of the utilization of inner light for healing, see Jane E. Latimer, *The Healing Power of Inner Light-Fire* (Denver: LivingQuest, 1990).

the complex interweavings of the form of this conditioned web. Now you understand it. You see it. You know where it is. "Finally," you think, " I can do something about it!"

This is how inner light works. You shine light into the nooks and crannies of unconsciousness and become conscious. When you focus light within, whatever is not part of Self will be revealed.

We can use the light to help locate and heal the injuries hidden within the events that trigger emotional eating. And, we can use the light to dissolve the defensive character styles of our compulsive self. There are many ways to connect with this healing power, but always, the healing energy is harnessed to reveal the blocks and release them.[2]

"Okay, Stacy, close your eyes and breathe. Move with your aware-ness into the radiance of your healing power—full of light, infinite love and wisdom."

Silence as we both soften into this safe and warm environment. "Now, invite your compulsive self into this space for healing. Let her know that in this place nothing will be taken from her. She is safe here."

Time expands — moments lengthen and we enter this new time, an inner time of healing.

"Go into the pain, Stacy, right into the center of the pain."

"She's a child . . . in the playpen. She can't get out. She's angry and very hurt. She cries for food because it's better than being trapped in there alone." Stacy's face distorts. The agitation moves from her hands up into her chest. She begins to cry.

"What does she need?"

"Love. She wants to come out and be held . . . I am picking her up. She likes this . . . now she's becoming stiff like she's not sure she really wants to stay. She's afraid."

"Of what?"

"I don't know."

Stacy is quiet. I let her be with her inner self to experience the light. The healing power has the uncanny ability to reveal and heal. It illumines what

---

[2]IBP utilizes breath to achieve similar results. Lightwork and breathwork are two powerful ways of harnessing the healing power.

is dark and unconscious. It brings love, power, wisdom and strength. It brings trust and safety.

More tears. "The playpen is gone but she has a pacifier and she won't let it go. She wants to but is afraid of being alone. She needs her pacifier to keep her safe."

"She can keep it," I say softly, "This is not the time to let it go."

We are quiet for a long while.

"Now direct the healing power into the spaces of her little body."

There is a breath, a release.

"She and I are embracing. I've tied the pacifier around her neck so she'll have it when she needs it. I'm throwing the crackers and sugar, the fear of being alone, into the light. I can't ever be alone. I have my higher power and I have my child. We all have each other. I'll never be alone!"

When we access our healing power, there can be a mysterious unfolding in which compulsive self is absorbed into the vast being-ness of the Self. As Self is strengthened and balanced, and as it seeks greater expression, the adaptive self slowly loses its power.

The following inner processes can help you access your healing power. Use them to help you locate the injuries hidden within the events that trigger emotional eating, to heal the fragmentation that has resulted from those injuries, and to dissolve the defensive character styles of your compulsive self.

Basic Light Meditation[3]

Before doing this meditation, be sure to read the warning for dissociative disorders in footnote number three below.

---

[3]Find this meditation on the audiotape "Inner Light Meditation" (#1 of the Filling the Void series) by Jane E. Latimer. See pp. 130 and 132 for ordering information. WARNING: If you have been diagnosed with any form of *dissociative disorder*, do not do this meditation without consulting your therapist. If you find it difficult or uncomfortable to rise up out of your body, think of the sun expanding outward from your heart area until your whole body is surrounded in light. Do not do the downpour. Just think of intensifying the healing energy throughout the areas of your body — allowing every cell and pore of your body and every molecule and atom of your body-field to soak up this wonderful, pure white light-energy.

Sit comfortably in a chair, feet flat on the floor, hands on your thighs, palms facing downward. Close your eyes. For best results, take a few minutes to breathe deeply into your lower abdomen, relaxing all muscles and your nervous system. Move with awareness to your midbrain. From here travel along an imaginary line until you feel your awareness coming to rest at a place about six inches above the top of your head. Think of a point of light floating, expanding in size to approximately three inches in diameter, becoming a luminous, crystalline white star-sun. Think of this sun opening and showering a great flood of energy. Experience this luscious life-giving energy flowing down into your body and out the bottoms of your feet, cleansing and washing away all toxic debris.

Slowly and one area at a time, think of intensifying the healing energy in your head, neck, shoulders, arms, hands, chest, stomach, pelvic area, legs and feet.

Experience as this downpour of crystalline white light-energy pours out into the energy field[4] that surrounds your body. Let every cell and pore of your body and every molecule and atom of your body-field soak up this wonderful, pure white light-energy. If you wish, continue with the following exercise to connect with your healing power.

If you do not wish to continue, open your eyes slowly. Look around the room. Name objects and colors. Feel your feet as they touch the floor, your body as it contacts the chair or couch. You may want to take some time to write about your experiences and stretch your muscles before resuming your daily activities.

---

[4] Just as magnets and planets have a field of energy that extends beyond their physical structure (eg., the Van Allen belts), humans also have an energy field reaching beyond the body. Kirlian photography records it; clairvoyants uniformly report seeing it. Most researchers believe that it is an organizing matrix that interpenetrates the physical body. One of its primary functions is protection. When it is injured, the individual becomes vulnerable to outside destructive influences. Its harmonious patterns, if disturbed, will eventually manifest as a dysfunction in the physical body. Consult the Resources section (specifically, Energetic Healing) pp. 123-124 for further information on this topic.

Connecting with the Healing Power

Focus awareness on your healing power. (This may be a higher power, inner power, God, the Goddess, energy, etc.). Open to the love that emanates from it and think of sending love back. Focus your awareness on receiving and giving love, magnifying this two-way flow of love. Feel yourself to be part of a circle of continuous and infinite flowing of giving and receiving love.

Open your heart and feel the light and love flowing into your body through your heart. Think of light entering your blood stream, carrying love and light to every cell of your body.

Now think of the light flowing into every cell and neural pathway of your brain; into your eyes, nose, ears and mouth and down into the neural pathways of your spine and nervous system — opening to the infinite wisdom of this power.

From this quiet place ask for a symbol or image of your relationship with this healing power. Open your eyes and draw a picture of the image.

Dialogue with your symbol or image. You may ask your healing power the following questions, then answer from its perspective:
- Who are you?
- How can I be aware of your power, love and wisdom?
- How can I connect to you when I'm troubled?
- Can I trust you?
- How can I be closer to you?
- Do you forgive me?
- What are you teaching me today?

When you have completed your dialogue, again focus your awareness on receiving and giving love, magnifying this two-way flow of love. Feel yourself to be part of a circle of continuous and infinite flowing of giving and receiving love.

Open your eyes slowly. Look around the room. Name objects and colors. Feel your feet as they touch the floor, your body as it contacts the chair or couch. You may wish to take some time to write about your experiences, stretch your muscles before resuming your daily activities.

Healing Your Out-of-Control and In-Control Selves[5]

Themes of powerlessness and unfulfillment are woven through the drama of our inability to stay and be in control of our food and our lives. Each of us is different with a unique story to tell. Making a connection with your out-of-control self (through visualization process and journal writing) will enable you to understand how it protects you from feelings of powerlessness and emptiness.

On the other hand, many compulsive selves are in control. They look good, dress well, exercise and eat healthy food. These traits, too, can protect us from fragmentation. Some examples of in-control compulsive traits are caretaking, people pleasing, overachievement and control. Taking care of others may cover up the emptiness caused by our inability to connect to our own aliveness. Overachievement may enable us to live with the deep down ache of our own unworthiness. That is why many overeaters are driven to excel.

The following inner process may help you understand and heal your compulsive selves. As you do the process, an image of these selves may emerge in human form (looking like you) or, they may emerge metaphorically (as an animal shape, monster-like figure, and so on).

(Before proceeding, review the warning for dissociative disorders in footnote 3 on p. 71.)

Close your eyes. Do the Basic Light Meditation on page 71 and focus your awareness on your healing power. Take a few deep breaths and release any tension you are holding in your body. Imagine the last time you overate or binged. Re-live the hours before, during and after the compulsive behavior. Allow an image of your out-of-control self to emerge. Notice the physical characteristics of this self such as

---

[5]Find this meditation on Tape #4, side 2 of the "Filling the Void" audiocassette series by Jane E. Latimer. See pp. 130 and 132 for ordering information.

gender, posture, how it moves, how it is dressed. Notice the thoughts that occupy its mind. Especially, look for self-critical thoughts that have to do with being a failure, unattractive or rejected. Focus awareness on your feelings. What were you feeling before you over-ate? Were you angry, fearful, resentful, lonely, bored, nervous, empty, sad? What happened to your feelings during? . . . After? . . . Now look for the core beliefs that underlie your thoughts, feelings and behaviors. Does out-of-control self feel wanted, worthwhile? Is life a struggle? What core beliefs underlie its interactions with others. (Some examples may be, "If I deny my true feelings, others will like me." "If I'm good and agreeable, I'll be accepted." "Intimacy leads to hurt. Better stay away from others.") Once you have a sense of the self-perceptions, see if you have an insight into the basic underlying core perception of this self.

Notice how these character traits and self-perceptions relate to your childhood. How did childhood events help create these traits and self-perceptions? Does your child wish to tell you anything? What did you need as a child that you didn't get? What does your out-of-control self need now? Allow your mind to form a mental picture of this part of you — your out-of-control self.

Open your eyes and draw or write a portrait of your out-of-control self.

Dialogue with your out-of-control self. Ask yourself these questions:
- Why do you cause me to eat this way?
- What feelings are you protecting me from?
- What do you need from me?
- Are you willing to change? If yes, how so? If not, why not? What are you afraid of?

Now, close your eyes once more. Refocus your awareness on the light and on your healing power. Take a few deep breaths and release any tension you are holding in your body. Remember a time in which you felt healthy and in control of yourself and food. Allow an image or memory of your in-control self to emerge. Notice the physical characteristics of this self: gender, posture, how it moves, how it is dressed. Now, focus your awareness on the thoughts that occupy its mind. What is it thinking? Notice what it is feeling. Look for the self-perceptions that underlie its thoughts, feelings and behaviors. Does in-control self feel wanted and worthwhile? Is life a struggle, or a joy? What core beliefs underlie its interactions with others. (Some examples may be: "If I'm strong and capable, others will love me." "If I'm thin, people will love me." "I have to do it perfectly before I can relax.") Once you have a sense of the self-perceptions, see if you have an insight into the basic underlying core self-perception of this self. Notice how these character traits and self-perceptions relate to your childhood. How did childhood events help create these traits and self-perceptions? Does your child wish to tell you anything? What did you need as a child that you didn't get? What does your in-control self need now? Allow your mind to form a mental picture of your in-control self.

Open your eyes and draw or write a portrait of your in-control self.

Dialogue with your in-control self.

- What feelings are you protecting me from?
- What do you need from me?
- Are you willing to change? If yes, how so? If not, why not? What are you afraid of?

Close your eyes. Think of the light and focus awareness on your healing power. Ask your out-of-control self to sit on your left in front of you. Ask your in-control self to sit on your right.

Now ask your two selves to turn to one another. Sit still for awhile and experience their relationship. How do they feel about each other? Do they like each other? What are their likes and dislikes? Is one stronger? If so, which one? Are they willing to work together? What are their emotional responses to one another? Is there a meeting place? How would you describe their relationship? Let them know that this is their time to communicate. Do they have anything to say to one another? Allow a dialogue to begin in your mind, then open your eyes. Continue your dialogue on paper.

When their dialogue feels complete, close your eyes and ask these two selves to turn toward you and your healing power. Ask out-of-control self, what she needs to grow, feel fulfilled and at peace with in-control self. Healing power will give her what she needs. Direct the healing power into the spaces of your out-of-control self. Do this by thinking of the fire aspect of the light burning the blocks to Self that are ready to be released. The spaces of your out-of-control self that have been emptied of these energy blocks open to the healing power pouring in, bringing with it transformed feelings, thoughts, perceptions, and behaviors. Ask in-control self what she needs to be fulfilled and at peace with out-of-control self. Healing power now gives in-control self what she needs. Direct the healing power into the spaces of your in-control self. Do this by thinking of the fire aspect of the light burning the blocks to Self that are ready to be released. The spaces of your in-control self that have been emptied of these energy blocks open to the healing power pouring back in, bringing transformed feelings, thoughts, perceptions and behaviors. As this process completes itself, ask yourself what you need to be fulfilled and at peace with both your other selves. Healing power gives you what you need.

Surround your whole body and energy field in light, burning everything you are now ready to release. Think of every cell and organ in your body opening to receive the healing energy pouring in.

Notice if the relationship between the three of you has changed. If it has, notice how it has changed.

Open to an understanding of what in your life needs to change. Is living beyond the food game a priority? If so, what must be done to accomplish this goal? What lifestyle changes do you need to make? What is the next, smallest task you can do to start making these changes now?

Slowly open your eyes. Gently guide your awareness back to physical reality.

Answer the following questions.
- What have I learned about my out-of-control self?
- What have I learned about my in-control self?
- What is their relationship?
- Is living beyond the food game a priority?

- If so, what must be done to accomplish this goal?
- What lifestyle changes do I need to make?
- What is the next, smallest task I can do to start making these changes now?

Open your eyes slowly. Look around the room. Name objects and colors. Feel your feet as they touch the floor, your body as it contacts the chair or couch. You may wish to take some time to write about your experiences, stretch your muscles before resuming your daily activities.

Utilizing Higher Power to Heal Fragmentation
The following Steps Out of Fragmentation are the same as outlined on pages 60-62. I repeat them here to demonstrate how your healing power can be utilized to amplify its effectiveness. New insertions are **in bold**.

1. DO NOT try to be functional — DO NOT try to relate to people or to accomplish anything. Your only job is to attend to yourself.

2. Acknowledge that the feelings are triggered by old childhood injuries. DO NOT use these feelings as a basis for making present day "adult" decisions, or as a basis for creating "adult" relationships.

3. Know that this condition is temporary. It is not a reflection of who you are for all time. You will put yourself back together again and you will feel good again.

4. Give yourself permission to be alone to feel and explore what you are feeling.

5. Close your eyes. Take five deep long breaths into your lower abdomen. **Do the Basic Light Meditation (p. 71) and connect with your healing power.** Whether you have overeaten or not, think about the event or series of events that has triggered the onset of your desire to eat. Retrace your steps backward, as if you are slowly rewinding a film of your day. You may have to go back a few days. How were you feeling that morning? Then,

retrace your steps forward slowly, *staying with your feelings*. What happened next? Did anything make you uncomfortable? If not, continue to move forward until you locate the event that caused some kind of discomfort.

6. Open your eyes and write in your journal. Answer the following questions:
    - What about this incident made me uncomfortable?
    - What was I feeling? (Look for feelings of rejection, powerlessness, restlessness, anxiety, fear, anger, hurt, etc.)
    - Was I afraid of losing someone's love or approval? Was I afraid of being used or manipulated?
    - Did I fragment? If yes, describe how you know you were fragmenting. List the symptoms and the body sensations.
    - Is there anything about this situation or my feelings that resemble my childhood in anyway? If yes, describe. What did my child need from a parent that she didn't get? What do I need right now?

7. Dialogue with your inner child.
8. **Ask your healing power to give your child what she needs.**
9. Visualize your child and yourself receiving what you need.
10. Write the appropriate "Good Parent Message" (see p. 58) that was missing from your childhood at least 20 times in your journal.
11. **Think of light flowing from above the top of your head down through your body, out the bottoms of your feet filling your energy field with radiant white life-energy, love and power.**
12. Come back to the situation that has triggered or might have triggered emotional eating. Answer the following

questions: Does this feel resolved? Are my needs being met? If not, what might I do to meet my needs? What might I do to resolve the situation?

13. Bring yourself back to the present. You can do this by looking around the room, naming objects and colors. Feel the space your body occupies as it rests upon your chair.

CHAPTER SIX

Your Body Power

WHAT WE HUNGER FOR IS AN EXPERIENCE OF FULLNESS
THAT COMES WITH THE *PHYSICAL EXPERIENCE* OF WELL-BEING, THAT
ENCOMPASSES THE TOTALITY OF OUR SPIRITUAL,
MENTAL, EMOTIONAL AND BODY NATURE.
IT IS WHAT WE YEARN FOR AND WHAT WE CRAVE.

Compulsive Self: I am frightened.
Self: As long as you have the power, you will live in a world to be feared.
C.S.:   I am small compared to you.
Self: Yes. Give yourself up to me.
C.S.:   How.
Self: Name the fears, then release them.
C.S.:   How do I do this?
Self: Stop pretending. Feel the darkness. Move it through.
C.S.:   But how?
Self: Move into the spaces of your body and remember.

Because most of us have experienced *both* abandonment and invasion in our childhoods, the experience of being *in* our bodies is generally unpleasant. It doesn't feel too good to have people close and it doesn't feel too good to be alone. Remember, these injuries affected us spiritually, emotionally *and* physically. We cannot separate the body from our mind. In his book, *Who Gets Sick*, Blair Justice cites study after study which demonstrates the dramatic impact emotional climate has on such physiological processes as the immune, digestive and nervous systems.[1]

We know the reverse is true, too. For example, 80 per cent of people who suffer with depression can be helped biochemically. Specific nutritional supplements and anti-depressants affect our neurotransmitters,[2] which in turn affect mood. Depression is just one of the emotional ailments that can be affected biochemically. It would not be outlandish to speculate that the emotional states of our parents may have had a dramatic effect on the very sensitive and precise physiological processes of the fetus.

I am *not* proposing we heal our childhood injuries with a pill, but I am stating that unless you address body-mind-Spirit *as a whole*, you will be sabotaging your progress. If your fragmentation is in part

---

[1] Blair Justice, *Who Gets Sick* (Houston: Peak Press, 1987).
[2] Chemical messengers released by the brain to the body's 100 trillion cells which affect, and are in turn affected by, attitudes and moods. For more information, see Justice, op. cit.

82

caused by a biochemical imbalance, then I highly recommend you do what is necessary to bring that condition into balance.[3]

Because of our injuries, I have noticed that there is an inability on the part of overeaters to be present in their bodies — which means to be settled, open and relaxed enough to feel what is going on inside. This is not surprising since, as mentioned, most of us have had issues with both abandonment and invasion in our childhoods. Thus, the tendency is to want to conceptualize or "mentalize" recovery, to think our way out of overeating. When we are not thinking, we are either overeating or feeling emotional pain.

Although the tendency is to want to mentalize recovery, I am becoming increasingly aware of how ineffectual this process is. Many of us tend to think of boundaries as our ability to say "No," or assert ourselves, or separate ourselves from the needs and feelings of others. While this is part of it, few of us realize that boundaries are *felt* in the body. The lack of boundaries can also be felt in the body. That is why I have asked you to be aware of the physical sensations that accompany your fragmentation experiences.

Body boundaries tell us when we are hungry and when we have had enough to eat. If we are not in our body, then we can't know this. We allow ourselves to be abused by food. We have no power to say "No."

Similarly, body boundaries tell us what we are feeling. Sensations in the body tell us whether we enjoy being close to someone or not. Disconnected from the body, we can't know this. We allow ourselves to be abused by others. We have no power to say "No."

---

[3]One of the most enlightening experiences I have had recently is stumbling upon specific nutritional supplements which seem to increase biochemical balance and thereby decrease the frequency and intensity of the fragmentation experience. Although the information provided within the pages of this book is an important piece of the puzzle, if you are fragmenting a lot (by a lot, I mean many times a week), I implore you to consider that a chemical imbalance may be part of the cause. Consult the resource list at the back of this book for further information on this topic.

Because fragmentation is a physically experienced loss of Self-definition, it is crucial that we build the body experience of our boundaries in order to prevent and heal the fragmentation experience.

The Body/Mind Split

Mind: *If we don't keep working someone else will get the promotion.*
Body: *Leave me alone. You never listen to me. You feed me junk so you don't have to listen and I'm worn out. I'm giving up. I'm tired. If you don't start listening to me soon, you'll get sick because I'm not getting the nutrients or rest I need.*
Mind: *If we rest someone else may get the promotion!*
Body: *So what?*
Mind: *I've worked hard for this. This is very important to me.*
Body: *It may be important to you but what good will a promotion do you if you're laid up in the hospital with cancer, heart trouble or kidney problems?*

Accessing Your Body Power to Strengthen Your Self-Boundaries

The experience of Self is, in part, a body experience. When I speak of body, I am speaking of more than just the physical cells that make up the biochemical organism. I am speaking, rather, of the whole complex structure of energy, matter and intelligence that constitute the human form. This thing we call the body is known to be but part of a whole mysterious enterprise of incredible mind-matter, function-structure, energy-form interplay. And yet, most of us perceive and talk about the body as if it is a separate object, as if we are talking about a person or thing outside of ourselves. That is because we don't experience ourselves in our bodies.

And most (if not all) overeaters perceive this outside object (the body) as the enemy. How we relate to this object will reflect all the feelings and judgements we have about ourselves.

The core belief, "It's not okay to be me" which is experienced internally within the body as darkness and constriction, is also projected "outside" onto the object of our bodies — and the struggle with appearance begins. "My body is not okay the way it is." We yearn for an experience of well-being, but because we are not in our bodies and we don't know how to have positive body experiences, we think that "making the body look right" will give us the "I'm okay" experience. Trying to get our bodies to look right is part of the food game.

Even when we get the body we want, if good feelings are not *felt* in the body — the emptiness persists. Then we go about trying to get that "I'm okay" experience in other ways. We try to replace an actual body experience of fulfillment with any number of experiences which we use to make us feel important. Because we live in a goal-oriented culture, what we seek is utmost in our thoughts, and yet how many of us can say we enjoy the process of our seeking or what we have attained once we have it. If we're not in our bodies, we can't enjoy what we have. If we aren't in our bodies, we aren't connected to our Self. This is one of the major causes of our unfulfillment.

Even when winning the food game, if the connection between body and Self is not bridged, the compulsion will be transferred to another *object*. That object may be money, people, work, sex, drugs, alcohol; any object can become the focus of our search for fulfillment. Thus, it is possible to create a life in which food is not an issue without healing this split, but then we create a life in which people, money, work, or something else becomes our primary issue and the Self continues to be lost in the process.

Having built a culture with values predicated on becoming successful and important, we have developed an array of impressive and important technologies which, in turn, take us even further away from the connection with the body.

I remember one profound experience I had at a workshop given by Jean Houston.[4] We were asked to close our eyes and move backwards in time, as we literally walked backwards across the room, into our ancestral past. I felt the ancient spirit of Woman with her deep connection to life. Then, as we were guided to move forward in time, I felt the split occur. It was not a personal split — but a massive cultural split — as layers of asphalt cemented the split between us and the body of our Mother Earth. I felt that split painfully pierce the inside of my gut and chest. I cried a bit to relieve the pressure and then quickly went numb.

If we view our culture as a macrocosmic reflection of the microcosmic psyche of each of us individually, we soon realize that our whole culture's historic disconnection from the planet is a representation of what each and every one of us experiences as the body/Self split.

With this split comes a terrible consequence. Out of touch with the body-feeling experience of pain, we behave in abusive, neglectful and destructive ways.

Pain is a body-feeling that motivates us to change. Disconnected from the body, we may distance the pain temporarily. But, in the process we add new pain — the pain of the eating disorder, the pain of not meeting our needs, the pain of remaining stuck — on top of the original pain. Disconnected from the body, we may walk the path to

---

[4]Jean Houston, Ph.D., *The Possible Human* and *The Search for the Beloved*.

our own destruction and not even know it. As we begin to feel our feelings, to be aware of our bodies, it becomes more and more difficult to abuse ourselves.

Talk therapy alone won't necessarily reconnect us with our bodies.

That is what we've done as a culture for too long — sit in parlor rooms and talk. You can't *think* your way back to your body. You can't read about getting there and expect it to happen.

It's important to *physically* experience yourself. You have to open the spaces of your body and release the muscular tension that holds the crusted and worn out core beliefs and feelings that make up your shame, guilt and fear. You have to breathe fully into the organs and cells of your body and you have to feed your body nourishing food — food that supplies wholesome nutrients for energy, growth, repair and regeneration. Most of all, you have to change the way you relate to your body — for it is your body that holds the key to discovering who you really are. Your body is your Self-boundary, which means your body holds your healing power, your feelings and your needs. It knows *if* you are hungry or full. It knows *how* hungry or full you are and *what* it is hungry for. Without awareness of your body — you don't know you.

In order to live beyond the food game, you must learn to trust your body to guide your food choices. In order to create a life in which you are the master — not the victim — you must learn to trust your body-feelings.

In order to create a life in which you are manifesting your true Self — not your compulsive self — you must learn to trust your body-feeling-needs.

In order to connect with and experience the healing power, you must be in your body.

The Body-Mind Dialogue

The following exercise will help you to begin experiencing your body. It will also help you to distinguish between the voice of your body and the voice of your mind.

With a pen and your journal or a piece of paper nearby, become comfortable. Close your eyes. Allow yourself to feel inside your body. If this is difficult, you may imagine a little person traveling into the various inner dimensions of your organs. Start with your head. What is your little person aware of? Notice the body sensations — color, texture (tingly, smooth, prickly, tied in knots) and temperature (hot, warm, cool, cold) that best describes your experience. Notice if this area is tight and constricted or open and relaxed. Then, move to another area: your neck, shoulders, arms, hands, chest, stomach, pelvic area, legs, feet. You may also include your heart, blood, lungs, digestive organs, reproductive organs, liver, bones, teeth, etc.

Once you feel that you are "inside" your body, turn your attention to your mind. What thoughts are you aware of? Is your mind judging any of these sensations? Is it trying to pull your attention to other things?

Now, invite your mind and body to speak to one another. Write a dialogue between your body and mind in your journal.

Here are some examples from workshop participants:

Tom's Dialogue:
Body: (Numb)
Mind: Can't find you, body. Where are you?
Body: Go away. Don't come in here.
Mind: I can't. Where are you?
Body: (Nothing. No sensation.)
Mind: Don't know what to do with you. Who are you, anyway?
Body: Not sure.

Susie's Dialogue:
Body: Ache in gut. Afraid. Want to curl up and roll around on floor. Someone help me. Hold me. No one is there. It is dark and lonely in here.
Mind: You are always so dramatic. Why don't you grow up.
Body: I'm dramatic because I don't get attention from you otherwise.
Mind: Why should I listen to you? You're a pain. You're fat. You shame me.

Body: If you'd listen to me, I wouldn't be fat. It's you who eats too much. I know when to stop. I try to tell you but you don't listen. You make me fat.

Mind: I have to because you pain me. I make you eat so I don't have to hear you.

Body: The only way out for you, dear girl, is to start listening to me. If you don't, I will continue to ruin your life.

Ellen's Dialogue:

Body: Feel so open and light in chest. Alive.

Mind: If you let yourself feel this good, you'll be disappointed later.

Body: You sound like our mother.

Mind: I do sound like her. She was right, too. Every time you did feel good, something happened to make you feel bad again.

Body: I am losing my openness. My chest is hard and tight. I am angry, very angry at you. You and mother sabotage my joy. I will not let you do it to me anymore.

Once you start to become sensitive to the needs of your body, you will wonder why you never noticed it before. I have seen miraculous changes occur as clients become aware of the needs of their bodies. It becomes harder to overeat. As one client put it, "I just can't seem to override my body as easily as I used to. I'm more sensitive to how tired and horrible I feel after I eat a lot of sugar. Abusing my body just isn't fun anymore."

One way to increase your body sensitivity is to fill out the following chart at various times throughout your day:

Time	Event	Head Says	Body Says	What I Do	Consequences
3:00	Work	Keep working	Walk	Work	Eat a candy bar
5:30	Making dinner	Hurry. Dan will be home soon.	My feet hurt and I'm starved. Let's go out to eat.	I hurry to prepare our dinner.	Feel resentful of Dan

After a day or two, ask yourself these questions: Do I usually listen to my head or to my body? If I listen to my head most of the time, do I find that satisfying? How does my body feel about that? What do I think would happen if I chose to listen to my body?

Body Boundaries and Food

If you eat when you are not hungry, you have no boundaries with food. You let food abuse you. You let it overwhelm you.

What would a boundary with food feel like? It would feel like you are separate from food, that *you* have an internal power that enables you to decide whether you wished to enter into a relationship with this substance or not. And, you would base your decision to eat or not eat on whether your stomach was empty and wanted to be full or not.

In order to know this, you would have to be aware enough of your body to *feel* its hunger. When you have a feeling of hunger and when you are able to tell what your hunger wants — meat, vegetables, pasta — and when you are able to act on the truth of your knowing, then you have a boundary with food.

If you follow food plans, diets, count calories, weigh or measure your food — you may be learning something about quantities and qualities of food — but you are not learning to give yourself an internal boundary.

The Hunger Chart (p. 93) will give you this boundary. So, when ice cream says, "Come here and eat me," you will know how to turn within and ask your body if, indeed, it wishes to respond to the ice cream in that manner.

Without a boundary — without knowing how to listen to the body — we have no choice but to respond the way ice cream wants us to respond. Then, we are no different than a twig floating on a wave in the ocean. No wonder we feel so helpless and so out of control.

The idea for the Hunger Chart came from Susan, a woman who had read *Living Binge-Free* and had called me to share her experiences and get further support. She told me that she had been eating only when her body was hungry. She was losing weight without depriving herself of the foods she likes.

Soon after that, I was working with a woman who had become terribly frustrated. She had done years of twelve step and psychological work, understood her issues, yet could not control her food intake. She came into my office one day and said, "Jane, all I want to do is talk about food. Why am I gaining weight? Am I eating too much? How much should I be eating? What foods should I be eating?"

I had her keep a written log of everything she put into her mouth over the next week. I also had her write her hunger level before and after eating based on a scale of 1-10, 1 = starving and 10 = stuffed.

Then, I had her answer such questions as: How do you know you are hungry? What does your head want to eat? What does your body want to eat? How hungry are you after you've eaten? If you didn't eat when your body was hungry or what it was hungry for, why didn't you? If you ate when your body wasn't hungry, why did you? Were you satisfied? What did you learn? After one week of observing her eating habits and motives, it became clear to both of us that she was eating too much food. Most of the time she'd eat up to a hunger level of 9 or 10.

When I told her she need only eat up to a hunger level of 6 or 8, she was surprised. "It never occurred to me that it would be okay not to be full. That's scary." We talked about what scared her. "I'd have too much energy. What would I do with it?" Because she has many interests — she loves to paint, hike, be with people — it was not difficult to help her come up with solutions to her "too much energy" problem.

After a few weeks on this program, she is now losing weight and, perhaps for the first time, feels that she has some control over her food.

To begin working with your chart, whenever you eat, write:
the time: *8:05 p.m.*
your hunger level (1=starving; 10=stuffed; 5=satisfied): *3*
physical sensations that tell you that you are hungry: *empty, tired, spacey*
what your body is hungry for: *I want a steak.*
what your head is hungry for: *fish*

what you ate: *fish*

hunger level after you eat: 8+

physical sensations after you have eaten: *Still unsatisfied. Gnawing feeling in pit of stomach.*

If you didn't eat when your body was hungry or what it was hungry for, why didn't you? *Because I had steak yesterday and there is too much fat in steak.*

If you ate when your body wasn't hungry, why did you? *Not applicable in this case.*

Were you satisfied? *No. I still want steak.*

What I learned: *If I had eaten steak in the first place, I would have been better off.*

For the first week, don't try to change anything about the way you eat. Just observe. When you have completed one week's observation, answer the following questions in your journal:

- When do I feel the most satisfied?
- When do I feel the least satisfied?
- When do I have the most energy?
- When do I have the least energy?
- What are the most recurring reasons for eating when I'm not hungry?
- What are the most recurring reasons for eating something other than what my body is hungry for?
- What are the most recurring reasons for not eating when my body is hungry?
- How do I know I am hungry?

You may use the information listed in Tips for Losing or Maintaining Weight (see p. 96) to adjust your eating patterns.[5]

---

[5]If you are having problems with this, it is possible to consult with me by phone. See p. 124 for information on how to set up a phone appointment.

Hunger Chart

On a scale of 1-10, designate your hunger level before and after you eat: 1 = starving, 10 = stuffed.

Time	Hunger Level 1-10	Physical Sensations	Body wants to eat	Head wants to eat	What I ate	Hunger Level 1-10	If you didn't eat when your body was hungry, or what your body was hungry for, why didn't you?	If you ate when you weren't physically hungry, why did you? What were you feeling?

At the end of each day, review your reasons for eating when not hungry and check those that apply:
__ stuff feelings __ alter mood (stress, anxiety, depression) __ anger __ can't say "No!" __ time alone __ fill the emptiness __ Other

Separating Your Internal Critic from Your Body Wisdom

When you choose to eat a food that feels bad to your body, your body will let you know. That is a boundary. Ask yourself, how does my body feel after it eats a hamburger? A Chinese meal? An ice-cream cone? A chocolate bar? Rice and vegetables? How does my body feel after drinking coffee? Diet cola? Juice? Herbal tea?

Uncomfortable physical sensations (such as nervousness, fullness, bloat) can trigger the voice of the internal critic ("I shouldn't have eaten that. I am bad."). The voice of the critic within is usually an internalization of a demanding, critical, controlling parent. The "I screwed up again" experience is a distortion of your true Self. You have gotten your Self image from the way your parent mirrored you. You believed what you saw about yourself in the reflection in your parent's eye. To the extent that what you saw obliterated your own knowing, feeling, needs — your Self-boundaries — you will fragment whenever the internal critic takes over.

The voice of the critic can shatter your sense of Self — your true feelings and needs. In this case, your Self knows that you have eaten a food that doesn't feel good to your body. That is all! If you leave it at that, you retain your Self-boundary and you learn that "this food doesn't feel good to me." You can then base future food choices on this knowledge.

But, if you allow the internal critic to distort your self-image — "You never should have chosen to eat that food! Look how fat and stupid you really are!" — you lose your actual Self knowing. Your boundary shatters, you fragment.

To avoid this situation, separate your internal critic from your body wisdom. Know that you are experiencing an uncomfortable body sensation — that is all. Tell your internal critic to "stop!" Wait. Soon, (probably within the hour) the uncomfortable body sensation will pass.

The chart on the opposite page will help you to separate your body's response to the food you eat from your internal critic.

Food Choices Chart

Food	Felt Good to my Body	Felt Bad to my Body	Describe Physical Sensations	Voice of Internal Critic	What did I do about it?	What will I do about it next time?
[EXAMPLES]						
cheese			Bloated - heaviness	Felt depressed and guilty	I ate more cheese.	I won't eat cheese. If I do, I'll wait for the bloat to go away and be kind to myself.
Meal	Good... food feels comforting like I'm nurturing myself.	and bad... scary being full	Too full!	Angry that I ate so much. "You, idiot! Why did you eat so much?"	Nothing. I wanted to punish myself, but I didn't.	I don't know. Maybe I'll eat less or maybe I'll just see if I can eat a full meal and not get angry.

The more you stay with your body experience (even if unpleasant), the stronger your Self-boundaries will become. As your Self-boundaries strengthen, the food choices you make will be based on how your body reacts to a particular food. If cheese causes bloating, you will probably choose to stay away from cheese. This is not a diet because no authority figure is telling you not to eat cheese. *You* (and your body) are *choosing* not to eat cheese. This is a very different experience. Diets are based on external voices that have nothing to do with your internal experience. Choices based on body sensations that feel either good or bad are choices based on Self need. And this is what we are after.

Tips for Losing or Maintaining Weight

Eat only when body is hungry.

Eat what body is hungry for (or closest available item, i.e., chicken if no fish is available, or broccoli if no spinach is available. Not salad in place of pasta or ice-cream.)

Eat only when body hunger is at 1-4. (Try not to let hunger level get as low as a 1. Some people overeat after allowing themselves to get too hungry.)

Stop eating when body hunger level reaches a 6-8.

If you occasionally eat up to a 9 or 10, that's okay, but be sure not to eat again until you are back down to a 1-4.

If your head wants to eat and your body doesn't, DON'T EAT.

If your body wants food to calm or soothe anxiety or lift depression (*and is not hungry*), DON'T EAT. DO Steps Out of Fragmentation (see pp. 60-62).

When Hunger isn't Hunger

Most of us mistake thirst, fatigue and a variety of emotional needs for hunger.

When we learn to stop *assuming* we are hungry and really become attentive to the sensations in our body, our true needs become clear.

The following dialogue is excerpted from a therapy session in which Gina discovers that her fear of doing the Hunger Chart is an expression of a larger fear — the fear of meeting her own needs, of being empowered.

Jane: Gina, what I'd like you to do this week is fill out the Hunger Chart, eating only when you are hungry.

Gina: I can't. I'm hungry after work, but if I let myself eat, I wouldn't stop.

J: What do you do?

G: I go to the gym first. Then eat around 5:30.

J: Are you able to stop then?

G: Yes.

J: What's the difference?

G: I'm sitting at a table eating a meal. When I get off work, I'd be eating in my car.

J: Gina, let's do an experiment. Close your eyes and imagine how your body feels when you leave work.

G: My shoulders are tired. [She points to her chest.] I don't have any energy.

J: Ask your body what it needs.

G: It needs rest and then to do something. It doesn't want food. (She is surprised).

J: You've associated that tiredness with hunger.

G: Yes. But my mouth wants something hard — to rip it apart. [She makes a powerful ripping motion with her mouth.]

J: How do you feel at work?

G: Powerless.

J: You are tired. You want energy and you want power.

G: Yes.

J: And you feel this need for power in your mouth?

G: Yes.

J: Are you sure it isn't hunger?

G: Yes.

J: How do you know?

G: The emotional sensation is strong and I don't want any-
        thing in my stomach. It is definitely a need for energy and
        power.

J: How can you get that?

G: By exercising, which is what I am already doing.

J: So, you are already doing what you actually want and need
        to do.

G: Yes, I am. (She is surprised.)

J: But, your head says you are hungry and that you are doing
        all of these good things to avoid pigging out.

G: Yeah. It's like I'm putting an extra step in there because it
        wasn't okay to answer to my own needs and feelings in my
        family.

J: How could you see it in a positive way?

G: That I *am* getting my needs met. I'm empowering and en-
        ergizing myself and waiting until my body says it's hungry
        before I eat.

As you can see from that example, many needs are registered in
the body. Gina felt tired in her shoulders. She felt her need for power
in her mouth. Yet, before she had really paid attention to these
sensations, she assumed they were hunger. If you are hungry, your
body will know it and tell you. Your stomach will feel empty. You may
have low blood sugar symptoms such as spaciness, fatigue or light-
headedness. If you are hungry and you eat, the physical sensations will
subside and you will feel fulfilled. However, if you are not hungry and
you eat, chances are the physical sensations will not be alleviated.
You will still feel unfulfilled.

Learning to distinguish between physical sensations is important. I have one client who registers anxiety as nausea. She consistently mistakes the nausea for hunger, then eats. Anxiety is an

uncomfortable feeling that *can* be soothed with food. But, look at the consequences. She is forty-five pounds overweight.

Another client consistently tries to relieve a constricted sensation in her throat by purging. While temporarily helpful, the sensation inevitably returns. Because body areas often hold states of tension that block the natural flow of energy, finding a body-oriented psychotherapist can help release the physical blocks that may be causing such discomfort.

As you begin connecting with your body, you may feel tired frequently. Many overeaters ignore the body's need for rest or energy because they simply don't know what to do. Lack of energy may be an indication that you are not getting enough rest, oxygen, or nutrients. If breathing is shallow (very common in people who are not in their bodies), you probably aren't getting enough oxygen. Breathwork and aerobic exercise can help you with this. If your digestive system is not functioning well (very common in people with eating disorders), you may need to supplement your diet with nutrients that can help rebalance a malfunctioning digestive system.

If you are confusing other physical sensations for hunger, find a quiet spot and relax. Close your eyes. Travel with your awareness or little person (see p. 87) into an area of your body in which you register a sensation.[6] Or, try drawing, or making sounds, or moving — allowing the textures, colors, sounds, or movements to express the body sensation. Don't try to figure it all out. Don't try to analyze it. Just be with the feeling — for as long as you can. Soon, the understanding will come — not in a head way but in a whole body-mind way.

If the sensation you are feeling is hunger, *eat*. If it isn't, determine the needs of this sensation and take action to fulfill them.

When Hunger is Rebellion

Risa walked into our second session mad. "My body *likes* to eat junk. I tried to talk it into eating salad, but my body would have

---

[6]Some people have difficulty feeling anything at all. If this is true for you, a trained body-centered therapist can be very helpful. See Resources, p. 124.

nothing to do with it. So, I gave it junk and felt lousy."

"Interesting," I say. "Let's do some sleuthing. I'll talk to your body."

Risa closes her eyes. Soon, she is relaxed enough for me to ask her to connect with her body. She becomes the voice of her body in our dialogue.

"What is it about eating salad you don't like?" I ask.

"I feel deprived. I *have* to eat salad while everyone else gets to eat a hamburger and fries!"

This doesn't surprise me. The typical American diet is loaded with foods lacking in nutrition. Some junk food consumers pay a price with body fat, but that isn't the only price we pay: high cholesterol, high blood pressure, heart disease, cancer, fatigue, depression are but some of the many other symptoms of a poor diet.

As we explored Risa's resistance to eating salad further, it became apparent that her body *actually* craved the nutritious food.

"Then why do you insist on continuing to eat that junk?"

"Because all my life, I've been told what to eat — first by my parents and then by the diet books. I'm sick of being good. I want to eat the way *I* want to eat."

I laughed, "But you just said you want to eat salad!"

"I do. But I *won't*. Not if it's the healthy thing to do!"

"Oh, so you're rebelling."

"You bet. I've had it with everyone telling me what, when and how much to eat."

"Now, you're sounding like a rebellious child."

"I am."

"How old are you?"

"Eight."

When children are given the power to make their own decisions about what they will and will not eat, they learn to trust their own body, and base future food choices on the consequences of their *own* learning.

This was clearly demonstrated to me one afternoon at a local amusement park. Jesse, my then six year old son, announced he wanted a caramel coated apple. They were huge. I bit my tongue and bought him one anyway. He ate about half, then handed it back to me. What a simple example of body boundaries. A child who is given permission to choose what and how much he gets to eat, will simply obey the dictates of his own body.

If, on the other hand, children are told what they can and cannot eat, food choices may become confused with their need to separate from the parent. What they *choose* to eat may not be what they *want* to eat.

If I had said, "Jesse, that apple is huge. Eat only half and save the rest until tomorrow," he would have missed the opportunity to regulate himself. He might, in fact, have eaten the whole thing just to prove that he was different from me.

Many overeaters must learn to distinguish between the voice of authority, the voice of the rebel- child and the voice of the body.

The rebel-child bases food choices on notions such as "You can't tell me what to do!" or "I'll eat anything I want to eat even if it hurts me in the process!" The rebel-child is *not* connected with her body because she is too busy reacting to the parent. Her choices are based on anger and resentment, not on true Self needs. If you choose to obey the voice of your rebel-child, you may learn (the hard way) that poor food choices can or will result in weight gain and poor health.

· The voice of authority is your parent. This voice is usually projected outside of yourself onto doctors, nutritionists and self-help diet books or is experienced internally as the critic and rule maker. If you choose to obey the voice of authority, you will probably continue to feel empty, deprived, unfulfilled, angry and resentful.

The voice of your body, on the other hand, is you — your Self-boundary. This voice may be so small it is unrecognizable. But, as you work with the exercises in this chapter, your body voice will grow. As you learn to eat what your body voice tells you to eat, you will never again need to diet. This voice is wise. It knows what and how much food you need to eat to sustain the proper functioning of your body.[7]

---

[7]It is not my intention to oversimplify the physiological needs of the body. In truth, much of the food accessible to us is lacking in adequate nutrition. I recommend all my clients embark on lifestyle changes which include an expanded awareness

As you strengthen this voice, you will need to withstand the voice of authority ("Who said you can eat that?") and that of your rebel-child ("I want another treat! More!"), but eventually you will feel a greater degree of control over your health and your life.

The Adapted Hunger Chart on the opposite page will help you to distinguish between the voices of authority, rebel-child and body. Always choose (to the best of your ability) to eat what your body wants to eat. Use your dialoging tool to empower yourself. Dialoging with your rebel-child will help her to feel understood. Dialoging with the voice of authority will help you set boundaries with the authority figures inside yourself.

As you learn to choose foods based on the voice of your body, to listen with understanding to the voice of your child and to give less power to the voice of authority, your inner child will come to realize that she, too, benefits by honoring the body. As you work on strengthening your Self-boundaries, your inner child will be empowered to let go of her rebellious position and take her proper place as guardian of joy, fun and play.

Accessing Self-Boundaries Through Body-Feelings

I have a friend who is pregnant with her second child. This time she is pregnant binge-free. During her first pregnancy, she didn't experience any of the feelings that go along with the event — the loss of a child-free life, the fears, dreams and hopes for her child. She didn't even get to experience morning sickness or what it feels like to be round and womanly. She was too busy bingeing and purging.

Our bodies are meant to feel. It's almost as if we become pregnant with feeling and then give birth to their expression. Feelings come and go. But we have to be present in our bodies to feel them.

Feelings are sensations held in the body. For that reason, I refer to them as *body-feelings*. They let us know what we need and value.

If you are a compulsive eater, you have probably spent most of your life out of your body because you hate the unpleasant feelings

of the nutritional value of foods and ways to supplement a diet lacking in adequate nutrition. Consult the Resources section (specifically Health Priorities, p. 124) for support in this arena.

Adapted Hunger Chart

On a scale of 1-10, designate your hunger level before and after you eat: 1 = starving, 10 = stuffed.

Time	Hunger Level 1-10	Physical Sensations	Body wants to eat	Rebel-Child wants to eat	Voice of Authority wants to eat	What I ate	Hunger Level 1-10	If you didn't eat when your body was hungry, or what your body was hungry for, why didn't you?	If you ate when you weren't physically hungry, why did you? What were you feeling?

At the end of each day, review your reasons for eating when not hungry and check those that apply:
__ stuff feelings __ alter mood (stress, anxiety, depression) __ anger __ can't say "No!" __ time alone __ fill the emptiness __ Other

that live there. As a child, you may have left your body for many reasons: your parents were not present in their own bodies, feelings were not supported and named, or the feelings you were experiencing were simply too painful to accept.

When you begin to reconnect with your body, you may discover that some of what you feel may not be much fun — shame, guilt, fear, anger, loneliness and loss.

But those feelings are only the means to the end — what you have to wade through to get to the goodies — love, joy and contentment. Chances are, those negative feelings were frozen a long time ago — when you didn't know what to do with them because nobody showed you. To feel them was terribly confusing and never seemed to lead to anything positive. That's when you left your body and decided to overeat instead. You may have decided to leave your body in other ways as well, like fantasizing or mentalizing. Nevertheless, you left your body.

You thought, "What good is this body to carry around?" And you were right. It was horrible to carry around. (Some feelings *can* destroy us. Shame kills by eating away at the core of our identity. Fear, guilt, anger and resentment burden us with a never-ending downward spiral of negativity, blocking new opportunities for creativity, joy and love.) Your body was burdened with all sorts of negative feelings piled on top of one another, getting heavier and heavier. You may have been gaining weight at the same time because of all the food you were stuffing into your body to keep from feeling. And here you are now — perhaps burdened with layer upon layer of fat, shame, fear, guilt, loneliness, grief or anger.

That's the bad news. And that is as bad as it gets. Here's the good news:

You were never meant to carry around those negative feelings. You were meant to feel them, grow from them and pass them on. Just like food. Eat, grow and pass it on. Not hold onto it.

I don't care how much fat, shame, fear, guilt, anger, loneliness and grief you are carrying — you can pass it all on through and come back to love.

To do this, you must understand that you are entitled to be open and alive (it is your birthright) and your body is, was and always will be your friend. But the hard part is you have to be willing to re-enter your body and that means feel the child feelings you've been avoiding all these years. If you had been allowed to feel them, express them and release them, you wouldn't have to be doing all this now! But you weren't. You have to backtrack, clean house, feel the old stuff and move it through so you can catch up to the present, so you can reclaim your sense of well-being that is beneath the garbage heap.

The problem with most feeling release work, is you can get lost in the feelings. You get stuck in the garbage. Who wants that? Who wants to wallow in a heap of shame, fear or anger? **It is only important to connect with these feelings so that they can be released.** Your goal is to get to an internal experience of well-being and power. That means to live in the present as an adult — to realize that your adult Self is in control, not your child.

The old feelings (or all feelings for that matter) can't make you do anything you don't want to do. Anger doesn't mean you have permission to be abusive to yourself or to anyone else. Although shame feels bad, it doesn't mean you *are* bad. Fear need not paralyze you. What you do with your feelings is up to you. You can use them to help yourself grow or to destroy yourself.

True healing brings you into the old feelings so you can use them for growth, then move through them and experience the joy that is at the center of Self. Sometimes this happens immediately. Sometimes it takes months, maybe longer, to feel the joy. But, if you remember why you are mucking around in all that mess — to get to the joy and really *feel* the joy in your body — (not just *think* you are happy) then you will have the strength to carry on — to stop using food to stuff the feeling, no matter how awful the feeling is.

Stuffing doesn't make it better. Stuffing just stuffs your Self down deeper into an already-stuffed body. As you learn to stop stuffing and openly be with your feelings, your body will begin to feel more alive. You will have a great deal more vitality and energy. Your health will improve and you may even begin to lose weight. Certainly, you will begin to have a sense of who you are. By owning your feelings, you put yourself in charge — for it is your Self that has the power to choose how you wish to respond to those feelings.

Body Feelings and Fragmentation

Breaking through the barriers that stand between us and our body-feelings may be painful — incest, physical abuse, overcontrolling or absentee parents are some of the original family scenarios that may have caused you to leave your body in the first place. Reconnecting with body-feelings can release painful childhood memories that may cause fragmentation. With the proper outside support — professional psychotherapy, support groups and/or twelve-step groups — and the Steps Out of Fragmentation, you can use these painful experiences to truly heal.

This is true for Laura, a successful physician. Her family believed that feelings were a sign of weakness. Feeling was simply not okay and resulted in her parents' rejection of her. As Laura works the Steps Out of Fragmentation (giving herself the missing messages "I see you and I hear you." "I'll love you even if you are different from me." and "I'll be there for you always, even when you feel.") and as she broadens her support network, she is learning to tolerate a greater degree of feeling sensation.

Because emotional eating is a coping tool — one that has been adopted to prevent the loss of Self-definition — it is important to connect with your strengths and seek support *before* attempting to connect with body feelings.

When participants first attend the Healing Emotional Eating seminar, they are asked to do three things: the Steps Out of Fragmentation (pp. 60-62), the Hunger Charts (pp. 93 and 103) and the Feelings Worksheet (pp. 107-108). The Feelings Worksheet will help you connect with body feelings on an ongoing basis. At least half of all binges occur because small, unnoticed feelings build until they finally erupt. Often, fragmented states are caused by the single straw that finally breaks the camel's back. I hear this complaint over and over again: "Jane, before I know it, I'm into the food. It happens so quickly, I don't have time to write in my journal."

Doing the Feelings Worksheet daily will prevent most of these types of binges.

Feelings Worksheet

Once you have the proper outside support in place and have reviewed the warning for dissociative disorders (see p. 71, footnote 3), do these exercises on a daily basis.

Exercise I

At the end of each day, prepare a space in which to be alone. If you are not in touch with what you are feeling, move with awareness into specific areas of your body. Pay attention to your body sensations — especially around your gut, heart, throat and jaw. These parts of the body tend to hold a lot of feeling. Notice if the area feels dark or light, open and relaxed, or tight and constricted? What color, texture, sound do you associate with this sensation? Does it have a feeling name? If so, what is the feeling? How does this feeling want to express? Does it want to cry, laugh, scream?

Go with its expression in whichever way feels appropriate. You may want to write, draw, move or make sounds. What happens to the sensation in your body as you express it? Does it change? Does it move to another area?

Open your eyes and complete the following in your journal:
- Did anything happen during the day to trigger this feeling? If yes, describe.
- What memories, if any, are associated with this feeling?
- What thoughts accompany this feeling?
- Is there anything scary about this feeling?
- Dialogue with your feeling.

Exercise II

(This exercise may be done in place of the one above.)
Do the Basic Light Meditation on page 71.
With your mind, scan the events of your day. What body-feeling

sensations are you aware of? What events are associated with these feelings?

Open your eyes and complete the following in your journal:
- Describe the events and associated body sensations.
- Is there anything uncomfortable about this? If yes, describe.
- Did anything happen to upset me? If yes, describe.
- How did I handle it?
- Does it feel resolved?
- What needs to be done to resolve it?
- Are my needs being met? Describe.
- Am I using food to handle this issue or feeling? Have I used food to handle a similar issue or feeling in the past? If yes, describe.

CHAPTER SEVEN

Creating
Self-Boundaries

No person, place, thing or condition
can take the place of Self-discovery.
That is the greatest
and noblest journey of all.

Food addiction is one of the most difficult addictions to conquer because we cannot abstain from food completely. Some programs suggest we deal with this issue by implementing strict *external* controls. These programs are missing one of the most crucial causes of the problem — that of poor *internal* Self-definition. If we try to band-aid our food problem by substituting external controls (weighing, measuring, calorie counting and so on), we will never acquire the boundaries we need and will always be a slave to such programs. If you really want to be free to live beyond the food game, it will be necessary for you to create strong Self-boundaries.

You cannot have Self-boundaries without an experience of Self. As you have probably gathered, this Self-experience may take time and a considerable amount of effort to acquire. The Self grows as we learn to listen, act upon and thereby trust our inner experiences as they are perceived through our body-feelings. It is fine-tuned as we learn to access, open to and utilize our healing powers. Healthy boundaries (Self-boundaries) allow us to have our feelings and needs in relationship, while allowing others to have feelings and needs in relationship with us. They are flexible and changing. When we don't have healthy boundaries we feel powerless in our relationships as well as in relationship to food.

In order to have a healthy relationship to food, it is necessary we learn to self-regulate — to honor our body's wisdom when it comes to food, while honoring our own feelings and needs in relationship. The previous chapter, Your Body Power, has given you specific tools for creating Self-boundaries in relationship to food and feelings. The exercises in this chapter will help you to further define yourself, especially in relationship to parents and friends.

Establishing Your Own Boundary

(Before doing this meditation, read the warning for dissociative disorders on p. 71, footnote 3.)

Close your eyes. Do the Basic Light Meditation on page 71.

Move with awareness beyond your physical body and see if you can intuit how far your energy body extends out from your skin. Now think of protecting your energy field with light. Visualize the light intensifying along the outer edges of your field — forming a protective shield.

Be aware if your energy or any part of your energy is leaking out beyond this lighted rim. If it is, think of drawing it back inside your lighted boundary.

Be aware if you are holding onto anyone else's energy and if you are, release their energy back to them. Let yourself explore the rim, traveling around the circumference with your awareness. Are there any holes or openings? Is it well sealed? Wherever you find a break in the rim, think of patching it, and then seal it over with light. Once all the openings have been sealed, intensify the light on the rim.

Sit still with this experience of your Self for as long as you like before opening your eyes.

Separating from Parents

Inner child healing is about reclaiming our feelings, needs and values *in relationship* to the parent. It is about re-experiencing how we have given ourselves away to our parents and taking those parts of us back.

The inner child visualization process that follows will help you to establish Self-boundaries. Although visualization is a powerful tool and can bring much awareness, ultimately what is learned in this way must be experienced in the presence of another.

(Before doing this meditation, read the warning for dissociative disorders on p. 71, footnote 3.)

Do this exercise with one parent at a time.

Close your eyes. Do the Basic Light Meditation on page 71.

Visualize an image of your mother. Be aware of your feeling reactions to her presence. Be aware of the thoughts, feelings, perceptions and behaviors that connect you to her. (For example, if your mother was controlling, you probably feel anger or resentment. Be aware that although these feelings are appropriate reactions to your parent, they nevertheless connect you to her.)

Establish your boundary by visualizing a circle of light surrounding you and a circle of light surrounding your mother.[1] Separate yourself from her by thinking of your energy being drawn back from her into your energy field. Release your mother's energy back to her. As you experience this disconnection take place, be aware of what you are feeling.

Some people feel guilty when first experiencing the power that comes with this kind of disconnection. If this happens to you, communicate to the image of your parent that it is not your intention to hurt her, but only to reclaim yourself.

When we release what is not ours, we are finally free to grow beyond the concepts that our parents hold for us.

Becoming Aware of Your Own Boundary Style[2]

The following exercise can be done with a partner, in a group setting or with your therapist.

Choose a partner and sit on the floor facing one another. Decide who is to be Number One and who will be Number Two. Close your eyes. Turn your attention inside your body. What are you aware of in your body? Do you feel your body at all? Can you feel yourself sitting? Can you feel yourself breathing? Where do you feel excited? Where do you feel tense? When you feel as though you are aware of your body, then open your eyes and make eye contact with your partner. Now feel your body. Notice if making contact feels different than when you were in contact with only yourself. Notice if you are breathing. Are you more tense? Less tense? More excited or less? How are you different now than you were when your eyes were closed?

Number One will draw a circle around him or herself on the carpet. Number One, notice if you feel different with a circle around you than you did before. Feel how you made your circle, how you made your boundary. Does it feel like it is the right boundary with the

---

[1] If your visualization involves mentally "drawing" the circle, a clockwise movement seems to be the most effective.

[2] Adapted from an exercise by Dr. Marjorie Rand in an IBP (Integrative Body Psychotherapy) training session and used here with permission.

right size? Is it big enough? How did you know what size to make it? Number Two, notice how it feels for your partner to have a boundary and for you not to. Number Two will now physically enter Number One's circle, nonverbally. Number One, what happens in your body when Number Two enters your circle? Number Two, what happens in your body when you enter Number One's circle? Number One, what would you like to do? Respond in whatever way feels appropriate. Both of you notice how the response feels to you in your body.

Number One, erase your boundary. Number Two, draw a circle around you. Number Two, notice how you have drawn your circle. How do you know whether that is right for you? Go inside your body in order to find the answer. Are you breathing? Are you excited? Are you tense? Where do you feel that? Number One, how does not having a boundary feel to you? Number One now enters Number Two's circle. Notice how it feels to be invaded and to be the invader. How does it feel in your body? Number Two may respond in whatever way feels appropriate. How did you know what you wanted to do? Was there a difference in your body or was the response motivated from your head?

Number One, draw your boundary again. Both people should have a boundary. Notice where your boundaries are in relationship to each other. Are you inside someone else's circle? Are you too close or too far? How do you know? Follow your body cues to know whether you need to make an adjustment to your boundary or not.

Share with your partner how it was for you. Were you aware of your body-feelings? Were you comfortable with having a boundary, or not? With your partner's boundary, or not? Did you like your boundaries close to one another, or not? How did the distance feel? How did it feel to have someone enter your space? To enter another's space? Can you see the way your feeling reactions relate to childhood experiences?

Maintaining Separateness in the Presence of Others

Because it is difficult to physically draw boundaries around oneself in most everyday situations, I have clients visualize a lighted boundary around themselves and around each person with whom they are interacting.

To do this, simply visualize a lighted circle or sphere around yourself and around the person with whom you are connecting when you first make contact and, again, before you leave.

Many of my clients say this simple technique enables them to retain their own feelings, thoughts and values in the presence of others and to leave the situation feeling intact.

Mirroring

This exercise will enable you to create a boundary, maintain a boundary and express your feelings and needs in a safe environment while in relationship.

You and your partner are to choose who is Number One and who is Number Two. Be sure the distance between you feels safe. Do this by noticing how you are feeling in your body. If there is tension, tightness, nervousness or constriction, then adjust your position to find a distance that enables your body to relax. Once a comfortable distance between the two of you is found, make a boundary around yourself by drawing a circle with your finger or chalk on the floor.

Number One will now tell Number Two how she feels using "I" statements. Two's job is to listen and to occasionally reflect back to One what he hears. Two is not to judge, give advice, object or try to change One's feelings in anyway. When One feels that she has said all she needs to say *and feels heard*, Two will express his feelings and needs with "I" statements to One. One will listen and occasionally reflect back to Two what she hears.

The following is an example of one such interaction.

One: I took Johnny to the park and a kid came up and threw sand in his face. My first reaction was to yell at the kid. I was real upset.

Two: (Nods)

One: And then I remembered a time when I was eight and this kid threw sand at me. I was humiliated. I wanted to hit that kid so bad, but my mom was watching and I knew she'd get me for that, so I didn't. I just stood there and took it — feeling humiliated and ashamed.

Two: Johnny had sand thrown at him and that really upset you. It reminded you of when a similar thing happened to you and how humiliated you felt.

One: Yeah. So, I decided just to watch and see what Johnny did. He ran after the kid, throwing sand back at him and then I really got confused. A part of me felt I should get up and tell him to stop throwing sand. But the other part of me was secretly glad. So I didn't do anything about it and now I wonder if I did the right thing.

Two: You felt confused and now you don't know if you did the right thing.

One: (Sigh) I guess there's no right answer but I sure feel insecure about being a parent sometimes.

Two: I hear it's hard for you.

One: Thanks. It feels good for you to hear that, and I really appreciate you not giving me advice, cause I know that must've been hard.

Two: (Laughs) Yeah. Sure was. Still is. I'd sure like to tell you what I would have done.

One: Why don't you? But let's reverse roles first.

[They redraw their boundaries.]

Two: It makes me mad to hear you did nothing. Everything in me wants to tell you, "You should have given that kid a good lesson." It was hard not to say it, hard to just listen and hear how you felt.

One: It made you mad to hear that stuff about Johnny and it was hard for you to not tell me what I should've done.

Two: Yeah. Because all my life people have told *me* what to do! No one ever let me figure stuff out for myself. That's making me madder. Why didn't they give me a chance. I felt so powerless, so unable to make my own decisions. Why, even yesterday I called Richard to ask his advice about the car. You know, until now I hadn't realized how much that still affects me today. I really want to start doing more stuff on my own — taking more risks — but then, suppose I make the wrong decision?

One: It's scary for you to make decisions because they might be the wrong ones.

Two: Yeah. But I want to try and I want to butt out of your decision making processes too — unless you ask me. That feels scary too. I wonder what's so scary about letting you make your own mistakes?

One and Two continue this process until Two feels complete. They may then choose to talk back and forth with each other the way they normally do. If specific problems arise, they will be better equipped to resolve them because they have given themselves time and space in which to explore their own feelings in a safe way with one another.

As you work with these boundary exercises you will begin to reclaim your Self — not just within the context of yourself, but in relationship to others. To do this, it may be helpful at first to work with eyes closed (see exercises Establishing Your Own Boundary, p. 110, and Separating from Parents, p. 111). Then, open your eyes and work to retain an awareness of your Self in relationship with others (see exercises Becoming Aware of Your Own Boundary Style, p. 112, Maintaining Separateness in the Presence of Others, p. 113, and Mirroring, p. 114.) The more you are able to experience your Self (hence, your boundaries) when alone *and* when in relationship with others, the less you will fragment — the more empowered you will become to live a whole and fulfilled life.

PARTING WORDS

There is no greater journey than that of Self-discovery. No other journey can leave us so filled with excitement and inspiration. So, too, no other journey can immerse us in so much loss, grief and pain.

To partake of this journey is to be human — with all its infallibilities, imperfections and mistakes. The great artists of all time allowed themselves to partake of and express through their art the incredible heights and depths of human joy and suffering. You have a choice. We all do. You can choose to partake of your life fully — or not.

If you dare to find support, make the commitment and act in a manner that chooses life — to feel, to need, to fulfill needs — you have the opportunity to join the greatest heros and artists of all time.

Once again, I wish to remind you that the material covered here is not the whole story. Changing food behavior demands a deep understanding of one's psychological and physiological motivations as well as a commitment to work hard at changing old, no longer useful lifestyle patterns. Although I have chosen to focus on one *very important* and little written about aspect of emotional eating, I do not mean to imply we can ignore the necessary behavioral, cognitive and biochemical approaches to healing that may be crucial for lasting change. There are many excellent books written addressing these latter approaches.

Whatever tools you choose, the results you desire can only come with discipline and a commitment to practice. When we first set foot upon the path of healing, because of our culture we tend to expect deep and lasting change to be mastered quickly. We worship get-rich-quick schemes, drugs and medications which soothe the symptoms without discovering and addressing the causes of our condition. Our goal-oriented culture undervalues process. Life to us is a series of climaxes. We focus on future goals: "When I get this . . . When I get that . . ." As soon as we arrive at our destination we are off on another journey to find the pot of gold at the end of another rainbow.

Yet, many of us never even arrive at our destination. Why is this? Too many of us are on our journeys with inadequate maps. If we think of growth as a straight line, we experience relapse as failure. In his book, *Mastery*, George Leonard explains that processes resulting in lasting change follow a pattern something like this:[1]

Growth cycles include a practice period, then an exhilarating spurt when breakthroughs occur, followed by a setback. Most of us seek the exciting spurts while tolerating, or even railing against, the plateaus of life. But, the plateaus, which require painstaking thought and effort, are the source of true learning. It is during these times that we either change our habitual and automatic ways of responding or not.

We have to *practice* the life we want in order to have it. None of us ever achieves mastery over any aspect of our lives without it.

This means we must be willing to *practice* what we are seeking day in and day out — practice connecting with our healing power, and doing the Steps Out of Fragmentation, the Hunger Chart, Binge Journal and Feelings Worksheet — even if we don't see *immediate* results. This means we must embrace the process, rather than focus-

---

[1]George Leonard, *Mastery: The Keys to Long Term Success and Fulfillment* (New York: Dutton, 1991).

ing on the goals. The process itself *is* the healing journey and intrinsically contains the rewards.

All spurts of progress are followed by temporary setbacks. People who have studied the growth patterns of plants via time-lapse photography know that when a plant growing straight up reaches the end of its current growth cycle, it contracts back approximately 25 per cent before growing further. Leonard identifies this process as homeostasis, the way systems — including human systems — maintain a state of equilibrium. Homeostasis (which psychologists call resistance) is a built-in mechanism that supports our survival.

Our internal resistance is proportionate to the size and speed of the change, regardless of whether the change is good or bad. If you are making big headway in your recovery, you can expect a setback before your next headway. This is the nature of growth. Two or three steps forward, one step back. Understanding this can alleviate the terrible feelings of shame, guilt and fear that feed the addictive cycle.

I hope that I have been able to help shed some light on an experience that can be so devastating. May this book assist you (as I have been assisted) in walking inward into the center of your truth. For you are here to live a life beyond the food game — to feel, to give and receive, to love and create!

God Bless,

Jane

P.S.: Write me. Let me know how you are doing. Your progress is my joy.

Jane E. Latimer
c/o The Center for Healing Emotional Eating
Box 101412
Denver CO 80250

GLOSSARY

Adaptive Self: A character style built in response to the family and social forces acting upon it — the degree and frequency of abandonment and/or invasion experienced by the child. Its purpose is to ensure our survival while living in an environment unsupportive to the unfoldment of the Self. It enables us to feel good enough about ourselves to carry on.

Compulsive Self: Adaptive self with compulsive character traits.

Character Style: Fixed patterns of behavior created by the individual in response to the lack of healthy Self-boundaries. The particular character style developed is determined by the particular type of injury suffered as a child. When the injury is primarily that of abandonment, the style developed is the Never Enougher. The **Never Enougher** attaches to people or other objects (such as food) for definition. Her greatest fear is that of abandonment because if she is abandoned, she loses her self-definition. When the injury is primarily that of invasion, the character style developed is the Super Trooper. The **Super Trooper** creates rigid defensive boundaries for definition. Her greatest fear is that of invasion because if she is invaded, she loses her self-definition. When the injury is both abandonment and invasion, the character style developed is the **As Iffer.** Her fear is both abandonment and invasion because when she is either abandoned or invaded, she loses her self-definition. One way to deal with the constant fear of losing oneself is to split off from the body. The As Iffer maintains self-definition by thinking. She lives an idea of who she is.

Dissociative Disorder:[1] . . .[The] disturbance or alteration in the normally integrative functions of identity, memory or consciousness. . . [The] person's customary identity is temporarily forgotten and a new identity may be assumed or imposed (as in Multiple Personality Disorder), or the customary feeling of one's own reality is lost and is replaced by a feeling of unreality. . . . This involves an alteration in the perception or experience of the self in which the usual sense of one's own reality is temporarily lost or changed. This is manifested by a feeling of detachment from and being an outside observer of one's mental processes or body, or of feeling like an automaton or as if in a dream . . . (as in Depersonalization Disorder); or

---

[1]*Diagnostic and Statistical Manual of Mental Disorders*, Third Edition—Revised (Washington: American Psychiatric Assoc., 1987), pp. 269 and 275.

... important personal events cannot be recalled (as in Psychogenic Amnesia and Psychogenic Fugue).

Emotional Eating: All behavioral and mental patterns of eating, restricting and obsessing experienced by the individual as undesirable, destructive or unwanted and which the individual feels helpless to change.

Fragmentation: An out-of-control experience of falling apart, self-obliteration, or disintegration, in which we have no Self-definition or Self-boundary. Common symptoms of fragmentation are powerlessness, despair, emptiness, rage, abusive behavior, and feelings of extreme guilt, fear and shame that interfere with functioning.

Injury: An aspect of personality development in which the growth of Self is blocked due to unfulfilled childhood needs. Where there is injury there is no Self-boundary. All psychological injuries are the result of some degree of abandonment and/or invasion and all children are injured. There are no perfect parents.

Inner Child: An aspect of the individual's psyche which hold's childhood experiences. **Inner Child Healing:** A process of reconnecting to our childhood experiences with adult awareness which can enable us to change our adult way of responding to the present day events in our lives.

Mirroring: A skill needed by the parent for healthy development of the child's separate Self. It entails listening, acknowledging, validating and responding in a manner appropriate to the child's feelings and needs.

Self: An aspect of the individual that lives in the present and is in touch with and appropriately expresses its authentic feelings and needs. It is alive and open to experience, holding the specific talents, gifts and traits with which it is endowed.

Self-Boundaries: An internal experience of one's feelings and needs as separate, as good as, and equal to the feelings and needs of others.

Split Off:[2] Separation from one's body in order to avoid feelings of pain but resulting in avoidance of all feelings, good and bad.

---

[2]From Rosenberg and Rand, op. cit.

RESOURCES

Eating Disorders
Breaking Free by Geneen Roth
Bulimia, a Guide to Recovery by Lindsey Hall
The Eat to Live Workbook Journal by Jane E. Latimer
Inner Eating by Shirley Billigmeier
Living Binge-Free by Jane E. Latimer
"The Living Binge-Free Attitude" audiocassette by Jane E. Latimer
Making Peace with Food by Susan Kano

Energetic Healing
Hands of Light by Barbara Ann Brennan
The Healing Power of Inner Light-Fire by Jane E. Latimer
Healing with Love by Leonard Laskow, M.D.
"Inner Light Meditation" audiocassette by Jane E. Latimer
Vibrational Medicine by Richard Gerber, M.D.

Inner Child, Recovery and Growth
Bradshaw on: The Family by John Bradshaw
Healing the Shame that Binds You by John Bradshaw
"Healing Your Inner Child" audiocassette by Jane E. Latimer
"Filling the Void" audiocassette series by Jane E. Latimer
Mastery by George Leonard
"Potential and Blocks to Growth" audiocassette by Jane E. Latimer

Journal Writing
At a Journal Workshop by Ira Progoff
Journal to the Self by Kay Adams.
The New Diary by Tristine Rainer

Nutrition & Health[1]
ABC's of Homeopathy by Evelyn Purser
The Amino Revolution by Robert Erdmann, Ph.D.
Fats and Oils by John Finnegan
Recovery from Addiction by John Finnegan and Daphne Gray

---

[1]Further written material on taking responsibility for one's own self-healing available from Health Priorities (see p. 124).

Rolfing by Dr. Ida Rolf
Solved: The Riddle of Weight Loss by Stephen Langer, M.D.
The Way Up From Down by Priscilla Slagle, M.D.
Who Gets Sick by Blair Justice
The Yeast Connection by William G. Crook, M.D.

Professional
Body, Self and Soul by Jack Rosenberg, Ph.D., Marjorie Rand, Ph.D. and Diane Asay

Organizations

The Center for Healing Emotional Eating
Box 101412
Denver CO 80250
(303) 789-9265
For a free catalog of books and tapes, to set up a phone consultation, to be notified of workshops in your area, to sponsor a seminar, or for help in setting up a Healing Emotional Eating support group — call or write the Center.

Health Priorities
Box 101412
Denver CO 80250
(303) 781-0771
The Center for Healing Emotional Eating's partner in educating individuals and groups in understanding biochemical and energetic imbalances and in making healthy lifestyle changes. Enables both local and long-distance clients to make appropriate food choices and apply specific, effective self-healing methods addressing the biochemical imbalances often underlying overeating, cravings and weight issues, fatigue, depression and fragmentation. A free information packet is available upon request.

The Rosenberg-Rand Institute of Integrative Body Psychotherapy
1551 Ocean Avenue #230
Santa Monica CA 90401
(310) 394-0147
Contact to find an Integrative Body Psychotherapist near you or for information about professional training.

INDEX

If you would like to sponsor a
"Healing Emotional Eating"
workshop in your area,
contact
Jane E. Latimer
c/o Center for Healing
Emotional Eating
Box 101412
Denver CO 80250
or call
(303) 789-9265.

128

The **Workbook Journal**

$39.95 (3-ring binder)

by Jane E. Latimer

With over 200 pages of visualizations, journal writing exercises, charts and information conveniently organized in sections, this specially designed, structured set of materials includes:

- Exploring Food
- Exploring Body Image
- Exploring Needs
- Exploring Feelings
- Exploring Creativity
- Daily Entries
- Hunger Chart, Progress Reports and much, much more!

Also included are instructions for many valuable journaling techniques. *The Workbook Journal* is the main text of the Healing Emotional Eating Workshop.

> **"Your *Workbook Journal* is fabulous! I feel as if I have a therapist or friend holding my hand while I recover!"** — reader in Quebec, Canada

Dear Readers,

My journal has been my friend and therapist since I was 11 years old. Throughout my recovery I used my journal to help me sort through feelings and work through problems. It is still one of the major ways I choose to deal with frustration, conflict and unhappiness. I've structured The Workbook Journal *to help you learn to cope with feelings and needs in ways that strengthen your ability to live free of emotional eating. It is designed to inspire and motivate you to come back to it over and over again. It will help those of you who are looking for ways to deal with life issues without food, have had problems keeping journals in the past, and/or would like to go deeper with your journaling processes.* — Jane

These processes can serve you long after food is no longer an issue in your life!

Audiocassettes by Jane E. Latimer

FILLING THE VOID series

From her own experience of battling the despair and emptiness we feel when we give up an addiction, Jane has come to understand that moving through this "void" is mandatory for recovery. By moving through its darkness we can release our false conditioning and thereby find the strength and power to be who we truly are.

#1 - Inner Light Meditation

A simple 20 minute white light meditation to use in the morning to begin your day, in the evening to end your day, or as a preparatory meditation before journal writing. May be used on its own (with no prior experience) or with any inner light healing process in *Beyond the Food Game* or *The Workbook Journal.*

#2 - Loving Ourselves Free

As we embrace loving behaviors and attitudes, we are free to let go of addictive/compulsive behavior.

#3 - Discovering True Self

Identify and release the false parts of yourself. Allow your true Self to emerge.

#4 - Uncovering Unmet Feelings & Needs

Learn to honor and respect your own feelings and needs and to be a responsible and nurturing parent to your own inner child.

> **All tapes are studio-quality Guided Healing Meditations**
> Instruction Manual Included

Tapes in the *Filling the Void* series do not need to be listened to in order.

Single cassettes @ $9.95 or $34.95 for entire series of 4 tapes.

Healing Your Inner Child:* Guided Imagery 90 min. $11.95

Side A: Core Beliefs & the Inner Child

Examine your past and free your inner child from conditioned attitudes, beliefs and behavior.

Side B: Cosmic Mother/Cosmic Father

Reparent your inner child with your unconditionally loving Cosmic Mother & Father.

Potential & Blocks to Growth:* Guided Imagery

60 min. $9.95

Side A: Potential for Growth

Experience the progress you've made & your personal potential for health and well-being.

Side B: Blocks to Growth

Meet, listen to, understand and embrace the part within that is responsible for blocking your recovery. Reclaim your power for creative choicemaking.

> *Recorded live at public talks and workshops. Although the sound is okay, these tapes are not studio quality. Music by Larry Hestand.

Name (Print Clearly):_____

Address: _____

City _____ State____ Zip _____

Phone_____
(In case we have questions regarding your order)

I am paying by ❑ check ❑ MasterCard ❑ Visa ❑ Discover
Acct. No._____ Expires _____

Signature_____

#	Title	Price	Total
_____	*Beyond the Food Game*	9.95	$_____
_____	*Living Binge-Free*	11.95	_____
_____	*The Workbook Journal*	39.95	_____
	AUDIOCASSETTES:		
_____	Filling the Void series (4 cassettes)	34.95	_____
_____	Inner Light Meditation	9.95	_____
_____	Loving Ourselves Free	9.95	_____
_____	Discovering True Self	9.95	_____
_____	Uncovering Unmet Feelings . . .	9.95	_____
_____	Healing Your Inner Child	11.95	_____
_____	Living Binge-Free Attitude	9.95	_____
_____	Potential & Blocks to Growth	9.95	_____
_____	Steps Out of Fragmentation	9.95	_____

Colorado residents *only* add 7.3% sales tax.
Shipping: $2.50 for the first item*.
Add $1.00 for each additional item.
[Enclose $1 extra, Canadian orders;
$3, overseas. U.S. funds only.]

Sub-total: $_____
Sales tax (7.3%) $_____
Shipping: $_____
TOTAL: $_____

> *For orders including *The Workbook Journal*: $5 minimum shipping within
> U.S., $8 to Canada, overseas $10 via surface or $25 via air.

❑ Please send me a free catalog.
❑ Let me know about Jane E. Latimer's workshops in my area.
❑ Please send information on sponsoring a Healing Emotional Eating workshop.

132